Daughters
of the
Fifth Sun

Daughters
of the
Fifth Sun

A COLLECTION OF LATINA
FICTION AND POETRY

*Bryce Milligan, Mary Guerrero Milligan,
and Angela de Hoyos, editors*

FOREWORD BY MARÍA HINOJOSA

RIVERHEAD BOOKS • NEW YORK • 1995

Riverhead Books
a division of G.P. Putnam's Sons
Publishers Since 1838
200 Madison Avenue
New York, NY 10016

Library of Congress Cataloging-in-Publication Data

Daughters of the fifth sun : a collection of Latina Fiction and poetry / Bryce Milligan,
Mary Guerrero Milligan, and Angela de Hoyos, editors.
p.   cm.
ISBN 1-57322-009-4 (alk. paper)
1. American literature—Hispanic American authors.   2. Hispanic American
literature (Spanish)—Women authors—Translations into English.   3. Hispanic
American women—Literary collections.   4. Hispanic Americans—Literary collections.
5. American literature—Women authors.   I. Milligan, Bryce, date.   II. Milligan,
Mary Guerrero.   III. De Hoyos, Angela.
PS647.H58D38   1995   95-19641 CIP
810.8'0868—dc20

Book design by Iris Weinstein
Printed in the United States of America
10 9 8 7 6 5 4 3 2 1

This book is printed on acid-free paper.   ∞

Acknowledgments

Our thanks go first to Moises Sandoval for his generous support and uncounted hours of hard work at his scanner and computer. Without his help this book would have taken years to compile instead of *a* year. *¡Viva Moises!* a supporter of Chicana literature from the early days of *el movimiento.*

Thanks also to our editor at Putnam/Riverhead Books, Julie Grau, who believed in the project from the beginning, and to Susan Bergholz, agent extraordinaire, who helped women like Sandra Cisneros, Ana Castillo, Julia Alvarez, Denise Chavez and others get the attention they deserve, and thereby has helped all Latina writers. Thanks also to Nicholas Weinstock, editorial assistant, for all his hard work and patience.

Y mil gracias to those anthologists whose work preceded ours, especially Cherríe Moraga and Gloria Anzaldúa, editors of *This Bridge Called My Back: Writings by Radical Women of Color;* Evangelina Vigil-Piñon, editor of *Woman of Her Word: Hispanic Women Write;* Tey Diana Rebolledo and Eliana S. Rivero, editors of *Infinite Divisions: An Anthology of Chicana Lit-*

• *Acknowledgements* •

erature; Roberta Fernández, editor of *In Other Words: Literature by Latinas of the United States,* and to the dozens of other editors, publishers, and scholars who have given of themselves and their resources so freely over many years to connect these writers with readers.

Contents

MARÍA HINOJOSA

Foreword

The first "U.S. Latina" writers I ever read were my friends—wonderful women who would pull out handwritten stories as we sat in their living rooms after a Sunday brunch or late at night after an evening of dancing salsa. These were beautiful stories about their childhood memories, blond-haired blue-eyed dolls, Inca goddesses, revolutions, and love affairs.

At that point in our lives, these Latinas had never had their work published. We were sure that no publisher would care about these voices enough to do anything but reject them. The stories were just for us then, to be shared and admired, critiqued and enjoyed, with laughter and tears over cups of *café con leche* and shots of rum.

That is a story of the past.

Daughters of the Fifth Sun: A Collection of Latina Fiction and Poetry is a groundbreaking book. Latinas and non-Latinas alike now have an opportunity to see the breadth and history of a tradition of stories and poems that were once limited to sofas and kitchen tables. This is a book that gives voice not only to the *madrinas,* the godmothers of U.S. Latina writing like Angela de Hoyos, Lorna Dee Cervantes, Rosemary Catacalos, Alma Villanueva, Ana Castillo, and Sandra Cisneros, but also to the goddaughters, the next generation of Latina writers, who are not only following in the footsteps of the *madrinas* but who are bravely and brazenly searing their own new paths.

I was the last born of four children, just a little *bebita* when political changes in Mexico caused my father's hopes of a job as a research scientist to evaporate. We ended up in Chicago, crossing borders in search of my father's dream, and suddenly the English Mami had studied in grammar school became the only connection between us and our new world.

There were lots of medical books on the shelves in the small living room of our rented apartment. My brothers and I used to look at the pictures and make up stories about all the bad things those people did so they ended up punished with swollen ears and lumps in their necks. Our downstairs neighbors, a British couple, had *Playboy* magazines that my brother and I would sneak peeks at. There were a few old Corrin Tellado paperback novellas (read: Harlequin Romances), with cover drawings of voluptuous blondes in the arms of strong, dark, mustachioed men. And then there were my sister's Archie comic books with stories about a rich brunette and a blonde wannabe who both wore tight sweaters and lived in neighborhoods and houses I had never seen before.

So I didn't do a lot of reading as a young child.

But that changed. By the late 1970s, my Latina friends and I knew of the male Latin American writers. We read Gabriel García Márquez, Pablo Neruda, Carlos Fuentes, César Vallejo, Mario Vargas Llosa. Years before that I had read one book in Spanish by a woman—a tattered book on my cousin's bookshelf in Mexico City. It was Elena Poniatowska's *La noche de Tlatelolco.* For years after I never heard anything more about this writer who had dared to defy the Mexican government and tell the truth about the 1968 massacres of student protesters. Only in college did I realize that Poniatowska was part of a great history of Latin American women writers. I began to read in earnest, from Sor Juana Inés de la Cruz through Gabriela Mistral. And finally I reached the contemporary women writers of Latin America—Gioconda Belli and Isabel Allende and, of course, Poniatowska. These women wrote about the countries of my roots and dreams, places where I had lived and visited, places I always hoped to go back to and stay in. But they had long ago stopped being my home.

Then one day a friend asked me if I had heard about Cherríe Moraga. Cherríe is now one of the *madrinas,* but back when I read her she was the first U.S. Latina I had ever heard of who had been published. A Chicana, a Mexicana like me, one of *la raza,* Cherríe was *filuda*—sharp as a knife. She broke all of the taboos I could have ever imagined. She was Chicana, political, a lesbian, and feminist. Her poems were passed among my friends like little notes you snuck behind the teacher's back. We were in awe. Cherríe was giving us a voice not only because she spoke of the search for home in a land that saw us as foreign but because she was taking on the traditional values of our culture. Feminists, lesbians, and outspoken radical Latinas were women who were shunned by our own "people." Cherríe was not afraid, though. From her gut, Cherríe was telling us (and my professors, and my father, and my prudish cousins, and anyone else who read her) that she existed and had a voice. Complex, struggling, critical, Cherríe was the first for us, but we knew that there had to be many more like her.

And yet, although I did identify with Cherríe, there was so much about us that was different. I was a Mexicana who considered Chicago and New York City home. Cherríe was a Chicana from a small California town. I am not a lesbian. Cherríe is. Cherríe was born in the U.S. I was born in Mexico City. I was so different and yet I could identify with so much of her writing.

Why? Because for me, what has been and continues to be my greatest struggle is to find my voice, my inner voice, my writer's voice, and to believe in it. Cherríe was the first U.S. Latina I was aware of who stood up and with her writing said, no matter what, *this is my voice:* What I feel, what I think, what

I say, all of it is important and essential and an integral part of the American experience.

That is the power of *this* collection of stories and poems. In every one of these writers I see myself and so many other Latinas who are in the process of finding their voices. I see myself in the woman who sits before a blank page and, without fear, tells her stories. When I read these *compañeras,* I am filled with trust . . . trust of my own words, of my own language, of my own experiences, of my own expression.

Growing up as a Latina in this country, I wouldn't say that I was raised with a profound sense of inner trust and self-confidence. There were so many doubts forced on me from the outside, because of language, looks, customs. I was the "Other." And for a child, being different often translates into self hatred. Inferiority. Insecurity. It was intellectually and emotionally bruising.

Reading other Latinas is and has been for me an essential tool in overcoming that painful history of self-denial. But how that happens is as complex and varied as the thirty-two writers who are included in this book. I never know what to expect when I read another Latina—what will she spark inside of me this time? So I approach each writer, as I did in this book, with enchantment and excitement. When I read the chapter from Julia Alvarez's *How the García Girls Lost Their Accents,* for example, I was suddenly confronting my own father as Sofía, the youngest daughter, does everything she possibly can to please her father, to reach him, to touch him, and yet he remains unmoved. On the other hand, the writing here can bring on a spate of sweet memories. Or perhaps it isn't even about memories but about *now* and the struggles of career-bound Latinas (so many of my friends). Often these *compañera* writers take me to places I never imagined I would go: To the bedroom and the sex of Emiliano Zapata, for example, via Sandra Cisneros. Or to the mind of a Latina child who speaks no Spanish, tormented and terrified as Sheila Sánchez Hatch remembers "being left in the old house alone with my *abuelos* and being frightened to death because I was only four and couldn't understand a word they said to me. . . . The terror of those syllables falling out of their faces."

Sometimes it isn't even the characters or the scenes that move me and leave me in wonder. It can just be a word. *Nada,* for example. Nothing. A word I have heard millions of times, the Spanish word nada is given new meaning by Judith Ortiz Cofer, and I suddenly realize the power of that one word. " 'I have nada. Nada. Nada.' I tell you that word is like a drain that sucks everything down. Hearing her say nada over and over made me feel as if I were being yanked into a dark pit." Or from Margarita Engle's story about Uncle Teo's retirement. "His kind of retirement is different than the American's. In English, you know, retired sounds like someone is lying down all the time, sleeping, or at least dozing off from time to time. But in Spanish! *Jubilarse,* you see? Jubilated. A chance to get down to the business of celebrating. In Spanish, when you are old you are wise, so that is certainly something to celebrate isn't it?"

In the case of Ana Castillo, it is a sentence that made me stop and think and analyze and remember. It's the first line from her story, "Being Indian, a Candle Flame, and So Many Dying Stars": "I left the parlor midway through the video about the Chamula Indian and his dying boy and told Eugenia and David who were sitting in the kitchen having a shot of *mezcal* that David took from his Buddhist altar to calm their nerves since they had both just been kicked out of a bar down the street for no other reason than that the bartender didn't like their faces and I said, 'I can't watch anymore. Is there any *mezcal* left?' "

These fabulous winding, multilayered sentences of Castillo's remind me of so many similar ones by Latin American authors. They are sentences I have always loved because they break rules. These are sentences like ones I used to write as a student, which came back from my teachers with big red marks saying "Run-on sentence! Please rewrite!" And with each rewrite, I would silently convince myself that the teachers were right. That these kinds of sentences were wrong and bad. That I could not write in English. That this was not my language and never would be.

But it's not so.

English is the language of these writers. They own it now. And it is in this language that these women write about home and belonging, about Mami and Papi, about countries and borders, racism and unexpected slaps across the face from teachers, about lust and sex, love and lovers, about revolutions and dreams, about gardens and barrio basements, about tacos, sopaipillas, *frituras* and tofu, altars and spices, maids, wives, witches, *curandera* healers, *putas* and virgins.

I may know of these things or I may not. I learn from these writers. To imagine, to create, to remember. They give me strength because I know of one thing surely that we do all share. As Latinas, we have all at least once been questioned and doubted. Questioned about our validity, our experiences, our language, our words, our emotions, our expressions. And yet we as Latinas have no ownership of these experiences. All women more than likely have lived through them. Which is why this book is really a woman's book. And if women's voices are captured here, then men should read it as well. It concerns them, too.

Sandra Cisneros once said that when she was younger, she occasionally felt as if nothing she had to say was all that important—that no one in her life, especially in school, valued her voice. Cisneros now teaches us about the power and intimacy of writing. "You need to write," she says, "as if you were sitting at your kitchen table with your pajamas on. When you are sitting at your kitchen table with your pajamas on, you have no fear, no doubts. No one is questioning your language or your heart. You don't have to worry about fitting in because you are only writing for you."

• *Foreword* •

All of the women writers in this collection have written for themselves and for all of us—Latinas, Latinos, and everyone else as well. For me, their words are like an IV, injecting trust and laughter and memory right back into my blood stream. These stories and poems keep me rooted in my struggle to find my own voice as a writer, a journalist, a Latina, an artist. I just remember them in front of that blank piece of paper. These women inspire me because they have taken whatever fear they had and made it into something so tiny it can not reach them anymore. They inspire me to write. And what a blessed gift that is. These women are inspiring a whole new generation. Young writers who will share their stories with friends over *café con leche* and shots of rum, and then know that the whole world is waiting to see what they have to say. Because what they have to say is important. Very important.

–María Hinojosa
New York City, 1995

Introduction

The book you are about to read is unique. Nineteen ninety-five marks the appearance of the first anthology of Latina[1] writing to be issued by one of the "major New York publishing houses." Despite the fact that there exist other, larger Latina anthologies from regional and university presses, this book is a milestone for a greatly underrepresented group of very talented women. Read on, and you will find in these stories and poems an abundance of energy, imagination, and high craft.

Until very recently, twentieth-century academic literary criticism more often than not described ethnic American literature as parochial, politically driven, and generally as being only a generation or two removed from a living oral tradition—all criticisms aimed, consciously or unconsciously, at somehow negating the validity of such writing as literature. But the worst criticism, the most devastating review, is no criticism at all, no reviews. Until "multiculturalism" became an accepted tenet of American educational philosophy, most mainstream critics turned a blind eye toward ethnic literature, whether Black, Asian, Native American, or Latino. What amazing works they missed!

This was especially true of Latina writers, who suffered under the double burden of an academic mainstream only just beginning to see its Anglo male hegemony crumble and their own *machismo*-oriented culture. Latina writers over the past three decades—that is, since the beginning of the Chicano movement in the mid-1960s—have suffered far more from invisibility than from critical censure. Obviously, the publication of an anthology such as *Daughters of the Fifth Sun* is an indication that invisibility is not the problem it once was. Yet the international acclaim achieved by writers like Sandra Cisneros, Ana Castillo, and Julia Alvarez does not mean that Latina writers in general have reached a level of acceptance on par with that of their mainstream U.S. peers. Latina literature is still regarded by most editors at the major publishing houses of this country as commercially risky at best, an attitude which effectively relegates all but a few "stars" to the obscurity of the small presses and literary magazines.

Reviews in large newspapers or national monthly magazines are hard to come by for small press offerings, a fact that is further multiplied if the audience for the book is perceived to be limited to one ethnicity *and* to one gender. In addition, problems of nationwide distribution and advertising have historically limited the readership of small press publications to individuals who frequent independent bookstores, who are willing to read catalogues and to special order books, who attend regional bookfairs—in other words, readers actively committed to seeking out alternatives to mainstream literature. That readership made an underground classic of Cisneros' *The House on Mango Street,* purchasing nearly twenty thousand copies when the book was available only from Arte Público Press of Houston. By way of comparison, *Mango Street* has sold nearly four hundred thousand copies since being reissued by a major house (Vintage Books). But the success of a single title was just that. Literally hundreds of other books written by Latinas from 1970 to the present day had been published by presses like Broken Moon, Caracol, Casa Editorial, El Norte, Fuego de Aztlán, Grilled Flowers, Kitchen

Table, Linden Lane, M&A Editions, Maize, Mango, Pajarito, Place of Herons, Prickly Pear, Relámpago, Third Woman, Tooth of Time, Tonatiuh, White Pine, and others. These have registered U.S. sales in the hundreds—a few thousand at best. The next tier up, independent publishers like Arte Público Press, Bilingual Press, Aunt Lute, Curbstone, West End Press, South End Press, and several university presses have also fought the good fight on behalf of their Latino and Latina authors, yet only rarely has any individual title achieved noteworthy sales.

But what are the historical roots of this group of writers? Where did they come from? Did this literature evolve, or did it just spring fully grown from *el vientre de la raza*—the womb of the people?

During the political and literary *movimientos* of the 1960s and '70s, *la raza* politicization ran headlong into the feminist movement, dissolving many Latinas' cultural and career restrictions in the fusion. Liberated, politically skilled, well-educated Latinas began to explore new directions in poetry, drama, and fiction, and scholars undertook a substantial reevaluation of the historical and contemporary sociological position of Chicanas.[2] At the same time, non–Mexican-American Latina writers began to emerge—women with roots in Puerto Rico, Cuba, the Dominican Republic, and South and Central America—rapidly breaking down what little stylistic and thematic homogeneity had existed earlier in the movement.

A body of literature and criticism began to accrue, and with it (especially in the Southwest) a growing concern over the apparent lack of a specifically Chicana historical tradition of literary, political, and social role models. The search was on, resulting in the rediscovery of numerous Latina women who had helped shape the American West. Yet, as critic María Herrera-Sobek writes, recovering a truer history does not necessarily mean that popular misconceptions about American history will be easily corrected:

The contributions of . . . early pioneer women have lain dormant in the pages of history (when not omitted altogether) and it is only recently, stimulated by the revisionist impetus of the women's movement and the Chicano Movement, that we have begun to accord them the proper historical respect and acknowledge women's role in the founding of the United States' colonies. Stereotypes are hard to exterminate once they have taken root in people's minds. And so it will take a long time to eradicate stereotypical images of [Hispanic] women that in no way conform to reality.[3]

Throughout the Southwest, a tradition of strong women did exist, going back to the very earliest Hispanic settlers. To begin at the beginning, the founding settler of San Antonio was María Betancour (1703–1779), one of the leaders of the thirty-one Canary Islanders who arrived in 1731. Known as *la pobladora,* the "foundress," Betancour helped lay out and name several sites in the village, names which survive to the present day. By the late 1780s, the largest general store in San Antonio (and thus the entire region) belonged to a woman, María Josefa Granados. In 1790, Doña María Hinojosa de Balli inherited her husband's estates and began expanding them. Ultimately she owned nearly one-third of the Lower Rio Grande Valley. In Santa Fe, New Mexico, Gertrudis Barceló established a saloon and gambling house called La Tules in the 1830s. Known as Doña Tules, the mistress of the establishment became very rich and politically powerful, surviving the Anglo incursion with style and a certain cynical grace.[4]

In all, some sixty Hispanic women held Texas lands granted directly to them by Spain or Mexico, and many others held lands inherited from male grantees. A similar situation pertained all across northern Mexico and what would become the southwestern U.S. Some of these land grants were dissolved by the Mexican government after the revolution of 1810–21 as punishment for royalist sympathies, but most were denied for various (and generally fraudulent) reasons by the Republic of Texas after 1836, by the state of Texas after 1845, or by the territorial governments of New Mexico, Arizona, Nevada, and California after 1848. Most Hispanic family lands were simply abandoned due to the rise of virulent anti-Mexican sentiments which lasted well into the twentieth century. An early example is that of Doña Patricia de la Garza de Leon, wife of Texas impresario Don Martín, and with him investor in and founder of the town of Victoria. Upon the death of her husband in 1833, Doña Patricia was reputed to be the wealthiest person in Texas; without doubt she was a generous contributor to the Texan cause during the 1836 war. Nevertheless, she and her family were forced to flee Texas when Anglo persecutors murdered one of her sons. The family's vast properties passed into the hands of squatters and the government. Stories of this sort are common from the Gulf of Mexico to the Pacific. The family of one of the writers included in this book, Gloria Anzaldúa, suffered such a loss of their generations-old land holdings.

Given this economic and political oppression, added to which is the fact of Anglo male domination of historical research and archival activities, it is not surprising that there are few literary remains from the Hispanic and mestiza women of the eighteenth and nineteenth centuries in this region. Yet not everything has been lost. "Recovering the U.S. Hispanic Literary Heritage," a ten-year project spearheaded by Arte Público Press and the University of Houston, and involving many scholars across the continent, has already unearthed several important manuscripts. The first fruit of this project is a collection of essays, *Recovering the U.S. Hispanic Literary Heritage,* in which Dr. Antonia I. Castañeda writes: "Precisely because gender, as well as social class and race, circumscribed the access of colonial women to literacy, their literary voice, with very few and notable exceptions, has been virtually silent."[5]

This silence forced Castañeda, as it has other scholars, to

resort to discourse analysis (examining historical documents generated by, if not actually written by, women) to develop a "socio-racial profile of mestiza women on the California borderlands" during the colonial period. The 1848 Treaty of Guadalupe-Hidalgo effectively robbed Mexico of much of what is now the southwestern United States, overturned long-established social, religious, and cultural conventions, and replaced Spanish with English as the language of government and business. It may also have forced a reflective attitude upon the subjugated population. Whether this is the cause or it is just a fluke of preservation, throughout the Southwest documents written by women begin to appear during the last third of the nineteenth century.

Nine oral histories of California commissioned by Hubert Howe Bancroft in the 1870s were by Hispanas and mestizas, a body of work which is crucial to our understanding of this time and place. At least two English-language novels by Californiana María Amparo Ruiz de Burton were published in the late nineteenth century. *The Squatter and the Don* (San Francisco, 1885) describes the feelings of the conquered Mexican population of California and the increasing oppression of that population after the Treaty of Guadalupe-Hidalgo. *Who Would Have Thought It?* (Philadelphia, 1872), also by Ruiz de Burton but published anonymously, is a historical novel of the antebellum North which gives a bitter critique of Yankee racism and greed through the eyes of a Mexican girl who was rescued from captivity among the Indians. Both works are extremely political, feminist to a great degree, and give a good sense of just how aware the Mexican residents of the Southwest were that their newly accorded U.S. citizenship in fact meant subjugation.[6]

It is not surprising that the first Tejana to achieve national recognition did so outside of the state. In 1871, Lucía Eldine Gonzáles (1853–1942) of Johnson County married the radical Republican journalist Albert Parsons, who became Secretary to the Texas Senate the same year. This radical "mixed" marriage was symptomatic of the couple's political views in general. Neither their marriage nor their politics gained them much popularity in Texas, so in 1873 the couple moved to Chicago, where for thirteen years they led various labor, Marxist/socialist, and anarchist organizations. In 1886, Albert Parsons was charged as one of the instigators of Chicago's Haymarket Riot but was never apprehended. He appeared voluntarily at his own trial, spoke in his own defense, and was convicted and hanged. But the fight went on. Writing as Lucy Parsons, this Tejana crusader's first published work was a poem in the *Socialist*. It was followed by a half-century-long stream of poems, articles, pamphlets, and books that champion one cause after another—and thereby chronicle her rise as one of the most prominent labor reformers/organizers of the nineteenth century and early twentieth century, originating the drive for an eight-hour work day and helping to found, among other things, the Industrial Workers of the World (IWW).[7]

Like many other Latinas with non-Hispanic surnames, Lucy Parsons was rarely recognized as a Latina during her own life, and as well known as she was among labor activists, it was only in the 1970s that she came to the attention of Chicana scholars actively searching for their cultural and intellectual forebears. But as Evangelina Enríquez and Alfredo Mirandé put it in their 1979 book, *La Chicana,* "The importance of Lucía Gonzáles Parsons to contemporary Chicanas cannot be overstated. With a lifetime that spans from just after the American takeover [of the American Southwest] until well into the twentieth century, she is a transitional figure linking the nineteenth century woman and the contemporary Chicana."[8]

Parsons' importance as a role model for Latina labor, civil rights, and political activists was also immediate, inspiring women like political writer and organizer María Hernández. In the 1920s, Hernández founded both the *Liga Pro-Defensa Escolar* and the civic and civil rights organization, *Orden Caballeros de América.* Half a century later, she helped to found *La Raza*

Unida and was actively involved in the crucial 1972 political events in Crystal City, where today a bilingual media center is named in her honor.

Several equally revolutionary Mexican women with U.S. connections have been identified as well. One of the best known is feminist poet and journalist Sara Estela Ramírez (1881–1910), teacher, editor, political and labor activist, and a founder of the *Partido Liberal Mexicano* (PLM). In 1901, Ramírez founded the Laredo newspaper *La Corregidora,* which she saw as a news link for Mexicans on both sides of the Rio Grande and as a more or less official voice of the PLM. In 1910, just prior to her death and the birth of the revolution, she founded the literary magazine *Aurora.* According to poet and scholar Inés Hernández, no copy of either publication now exists, and the "extant body of her poetry appears in the Texas-Mexican newspapers *La Crónica* and *El Demócrata Fronterizo.*" Her personal connection with Texas began when she moved from her birthplace, Villa de Progreso, Coahuila, to Laredo, Texas, around 1897. Until her untimely death at the age of twenty-nine, Ramírez based her literary, journalistic, and political activities in Laredo, though she often traveled to Mexico City and throughout the northern state of Coahuila as an organizer.[9]

Ramírez's influence, however, is surely limited to the example of her life and to the force of her political rhetoric rather than to any stylistic aspects of her poetry, which is rather typical turn-of-the-century Mexican verse, ornate and passionate. But politics and literature have always gone hand in hand in Latin America. Ramírez represents writers who work on both sides of the U.S.–Mexico border in the service of oppressed peoples. As Hernández puts it, Ramírez's life and work show "how the border often becomes erased when considering the experience of the Mexican people and in their response to domination and oppression."[10] The fact that there is not a single contemporary Latina writer whose literary work is devoid of political themes is a good indication that precursors like Sara Ramírez reflect an enduring *conciencia de la raza* rather than a revolutionary fervor limited to any one particular period or conflict.

Ramírez is also an excellent example of the many Latina poets who published almost exclusively in newspapers. Scholar Juanita Luna Lawhn summarizes the situation:

> Recent historical literary studies are document-ing and illustrating the influence of Spanish-language newspapers on contemporary Latino/Latina literature. These studies illustrate that Chicano literature is a natural outgrowth and a continuation of an on-going Hispanic literary tradition that has always been pre-sent in the United States, especially in the Southwest and in the greater Chicago area. Consequently, the theory often vocalized that today's Chicano literary as well as non-literary community has evolved strictly from an oral tradition is no longer viable. Instead, a new theory which states that the literary, social, and moral development of the Chicano community has been strongly influenced by the written word can and should modify and redefine the old theory of orality.[11]

Lawhn's work with *La Prensa, El Regidor,* and others of the dozens of Spanish-language newspapers printed in the U.S. during the first half of this century has unearthed a number of Latina writers of substance and power,[12] yet her argument for the existence of a "literary tradition" stretches the definition of tradition. Most contemporary Latina writers will cite any number of non-Latino/Latina writers as early inspirations and openly admit that they became aware of intellectual forebears such as Ramírez only when well into the development of their writing careers. On the other hand, these "forgotten" writers may have had a substantial impact on the grandmothers of contemporary Chicana writers. It is interesting to observe that the majority of Latina writers who came of age in the 1960s or shortly thereafter have described their female role models as belonging to the generation prior to that of their parents. Numerous *abuelita* poems and stories depict strong-willed survivors, women who had yearned for independence long years before the women's movement of the 1960s. It is possible that this awareness stemmed from growing up with the strident feminist rhetoric of various short-lived publications such as El Paso's *La voz de la mujer* (July to October 1907) or from witnessing the 1920s editorial debate that raged in the pages of *La Prensa,* a paper with an almost universally Spanish-language readership from Texas to California. This debate pitted the traditional views held by the paper's male editors against the emerging feminism of its many female editorial writers (notably Antonieta Rivas), short fiction writers, and poets. The community of intellectual Mexican exiles in San Antonio, known as *El México de Afuera,* became a microcosm representative of the larger implications of this debate. As Lawhn points out, "by the second half of the 1920s, the selection of feminist essays published in the '*Sección del hogar y la sociedad*' (of *La Prensa*) broke the silence of the women of *El México de Afuera.*" Similarly, the "*crónicas femeninas*" of María Luisa Garza (writing under the pseudonym Loreley) published in the Texas-Mexican newspaper *El Imparcial de Texas,* along with her feminist novels published by the Quiroga Company of San Antonio, were very popular among Hispanic women of this generation on both sides of the border.[13]

There are so-called undiscovered writers of the same period and status as Sara Ramírez, Loreley, and Antonieta Rivas—writers whose major works have never been translated or published, yet who will in all probability become major influences as scholars continue to delve into this period. Such is journalist and activist Leonor Villegas de Magnón (1876–1955), the author of *La Rebelde* (The Woman Rebel), an autobiographical novel covering the author's life from 1876 to 1920 which focuses on her role during the Mexican Revolution as the co-founder (with Jovita Idar, another Laredo Mexican-American) of *La Cruz Blanca,* an auxiliary unit of nurses who accompanied the revolutionary *Carrancistas* from Coahuila to Mexico City. A portion of this work was translated by Clara Lomas for inclusion in the *Longman Anthology of World Literature by Women, 1875–1975,* and finally published in its entirety by Arte Público Press in 1994. The narrative is indeed lively and well written, describing events of substantial interest. Villegas de Magnón was born in Nuevo Laredo, Mexico, but was educated in San Antonio and New York, married a U.S. citizen, and conducted much of her political work from Laredo, Texas, where she ran a bilingual kindergarten. She was a member of Laredo's *Junta Revolucionaria* (Revolutionary Council) and wrote editorials and dispatches for the U.S.–Mexican newspapers *La Crónica* and *El Progreso.*

The naturally radical inclinations of Latina scholars in their search for intellectual forebears has produced a certain blindness to the obvious in the case of the few Latina writers who achieved statewide or even national recognition for work which may, in some cases, appear to fit mainstream Anglo stereotypes about Mexico, the Southwest, or Latino culture in general. Thus the works of Jovita Guerra González de Mireles (1899–1983) and the woman herself rarely catch the attention of contemporary Latina scholars.

Born in Rome, Texas, González de Mireles earned a masters degree at the University of Texas at Austin. In 1930, she became the first Mexican-American president of the Texas Folklore Society—a startling feat when one realizes that in the year she joined the society, there were only two other Hispanic names on the membership roster. González's studies in folklore led her to collect and edit the society publication, *Folklore of the Texas-Mexican Vaquero,* and to write a collection of her own memories of life along the Rio Grande, "Among My People," which she did as a series of gently humorous tales focusing on individual characters. Originally published in *Tone the Bell Easy,* edited by J. Frank Dobie, these stories surfaced again in Charles Tatum's 1990 *Mexican American Literature.* Other studies by González appeared in Dobie's *Puro Mexicano.*

Jovita and her husband, Edmundo E. Mireles, established the state's first major bilingual trade-school program in the 1940s in Corpus Christi, for which they wrote *El Español Elemental* and *Mi Libro Español* (a three-volume series). According to Tatum, the books "have been used to promote bilingual education throughout the southwestern United States." A minor writer at best and a high school Spanish teacher in Corpus Christi for twenty-seven years, Jovita González was nonetheless a quiet revolutionary who broke ethnic barriers and overturned systems.[14]

An even more startling omission on the part of contemporary Chicana scholars, at least upon initial inquiry, is the novelist, short story writer, poet, and dramatist Josefina Niggli (1910–1983). As Chester Seltzer, also known as Amado Muro, was to Chicano writers, so Niggli was (and remains) to Chicanas—a "white" woman with a deceptive name and the "correct" geographical background and topical inclinations. Niggli was born in 1910 on an old Mexican estate near Hidalgo, Nuevo Leon, where her parents had lived since 1893. Niggli's father's Swiss-Alsatian ancestors had arrived in Texas around 1836, and her Virginian mother's people were of Irish, French, and German extraction. Thus she fails to pass the blood test—*la prueba de sangre*—to be classified a Latina.

This is, however, a very fine line to draw, and one which has caused considerable consternation among Latino critics when applied to male writers. In a seminal essay, Raymond Paredes offered the following definition: "Chicano literature is that body of works produced by United States citizens and residents of Mexican descent for whom a sense of ethnicity is a critical part of their literary sensibilities and for whom the portrayal of their ethnic experience is a major concern."[15] Claiming lifelong dual citizenship and setting all of her best work in Mexico among indigenous residents, Niggli seems to fit the technical requirements of this definition, if not the blood test. Even a purist Latino critic like Juan Bruce-Novoa has admitted that it would be "difficult" to "justify the exclusion" of Niggli from the canon,[16] though this is virtually all he has to say of her or her work. Co-authors Carmen Salazar Parr and Genevieve Ramírez, in a short essay entitled "The Female Hero in Chicano Literature," discuss several characters from Niggli's plays, and apparently accept Niggli as a Latina without question.[17] But isolated references and a single essay do not constitute critical acceptance, especially given Niggli's notable absence from other Latina critical works. The final straw appears to be the inclusion of Niggli in Charles Tatum's groundbreaking high school textbook, *Mexican-American Literature.*[18] As the first and only textbook of its kind, this book will, as is the way of such works, likely render the question of Niggli's bloodline moot by establishing a canon with or without the approbation of purist critics.

Niggli's first book of poems, *Mexican Silhouettes,* was published in Hidalgo, Nuevo Leon, in 1928; another larger edition was published in San Antonio in 1931. After studying playwriting for a short time under Coates Gwynne, director of the San Antonio Little Theater, Niggli went on to do graduate work in drama at the University of North Carolina, where she became associated with the Carolina Playwrights group— which included Paul Green and, upon occasion, Thomas Wolfe. From Chapel Hill, she moved to Western Carolina College, where she completed most of her important work and taught drama and radio production until her retirement.

Niggli's reputation was assured upon the publication of several one-act plays, especially *The Red Velvet Goat* (Samuel French, 1938) and *Sunday Costs Five Pesos* (1939). According to the publisher, as of the mid-1970s the latter work was the "most produced one-act play in English," and Niggli herself said that she could have "managed" on the royalties from that play alone. Of more interest to contemporary Latinas are her two plays *Soldadera* (1936) and *The Ring of General Macías* (1943), which show Niggli's revolutionary sympathies through her depiction of female heroes on both sides of the political struggle. A less strident and much more popular work was Niggli's bestselling *Mexican Village* (1945), a collection of ten novelettes set in Hidalgo, the author's hometown. MGM Studios hired Niggli to help script *Mexican Village* into the popular movie called *Sombrero,* which starred Pier Angeli and Ricardo Montalban.

Niggli's first novel, *Step Down, Elder Brother* (1947) received only middling reviews, and the author lapsed into silence. Perhaps her finest prose work, though it is seldom so recognized, was her novel *A Miracle for Mexico* (1964). This thoughtful retelling of the story of the apparition of the Virgin of Guadalupe to the Aztec peasant Juan Diego is a finely crafted book, illustrated with paintings by Alejandro Rangel Hidalgo, and much sought after by collectors.[19]

According to John Igo, a long-time friend of the author, Niggli experimented in the late 1930s and 1940s with "narrator, point of view, a double sense of reality, in short, some of the techniques popularized by others, such as Carlos Fuentes, Camus, even Beckett." Three short pieces of surreal fiction, part of a manuscript collection bequeathed to Igo upon Niggli's death, were published posthumously to back up this assertion. Doubtless, Niggli crafted her work very carefully, was well aware of contemporary trends in world literature, and is worth further study.[20]

It is thus quite clear that contemporary Latina writing does in fact have deep intellectual and literary roots, especially in the Southwest. What changed in the 1960s was primarily a political awakening combined with a massive increase in the numbers of Latinas and Latinos seeking higher education. For

Latinas in particular, the question of identity acquired a high priority. The first U.S. literary journal to dedicate an issue exclusively to Latina literature was the September 1973 issue of *El Grito,* subtitled *Chicanas en la literatura y el arte,* with Estela Portillo, a Tejana from El Paso, as contributing editor and guiding light. The opening words of her introduction reflect the Latina's assertion of identity:

> The voice of a woman? Does it belong to a particular time and place? Is it not something much more eternal? Like the womb? Is it a soft, gentle fertility of instinct? The gesture is new, but the roots are the same. A woman sings of creation, and of recreation. The gesture is a song that blends the common experience to the consistency of a complex world. . . . The texture of this particular literary expression is tradition. Here, a distinct point is made. What is tradition to a man differs in varying degree from what is tradition to a woman. . . .[21]

Within a short time, most Chicano publications had addressed the topic in some manner, and new, often short-lived journals devoted exclusively to Latina feminist perspectives began to appear. Yet a decade later, the goal of mainstream critical acceptance remained elusive. As poet Evangelina Vigil pointed out in her introduction to the 1983 "Woman of Her Word" issue of *Revista Chicano-Riqueña,* "Removed from the mainstream of American literature and barely emerging on the Hispanic literary scene, the creativity of Latina writers exists autonomously."[22] Or, as Vigil put it more succinctly in a poem, "it is damn hard making it as a Chicana in the U.S.A." Also by this time the nature of the politicization had changed: Latinas no longer saw themselves as simply the feminist extension of the Chicano movement, but as an integral part of Third World Feminism. Writing in the second edition (1983) of *This*

Bridge Called My Back: Writings by Radical Women of Color, editor Cherríe Moraga acknowledged that "to change the world, we have to change ourselves—even sometimes our most cherished block-hard convictions. As *This Bridge Called My Back* is not written in stone, neither is our political vision. It is subject to change."[23]

The period from 1983 to the present has seen many changes; foremost among them in this context are the number of Latinas who can call themselves established writers. National Endowment for the Arts fellowships in fiction and poetry, so elusive in the 1970s, began to come to Latinas with increasing regularity throughout the succeeding decade; major literary prizes went to Latinas; so too did important university and arts administration positions. Moreover, the writers themselves came to accept a broader concept of U.S. Latina identity. Gloria Anzaldúa, in her brilliant 1987 essay "The New Mestiza," wrote:

> The new mestiza copes by developing a tolerance for contradictions, a tolerance for ambiguity. She learns to be an Indian in Mexican culture, to be Mexican from an Anglo point of view. She learns to juggle cultures. She has a plural personality, she operates in a pluralistic mode—nothing is thrust out, the good the bad and the ugly, nothing rejected, nothing abandoned. Not only does she sustain contradictions, she turns the ambivalence into something else.
>
> She can be jarred out of ambivalence by an intense, and often painful, emotional event which inverts or resolves the ambivalence. . . . It is work that the soul performs. That focal point or fulcrum, that juncture where the mestiza stands, is where phenomena tend to collide. It is where the possibility of uniting all that is separate occurs. This assembly is not one where severed or separated pieces merely come to-

gether. Nor is it a balancing act of opposing powers. In attempting to work out a synthesis, the self has added a third element which is greater than the sum of its severed parts. That third element is a new consciousness—a mestiza consciousness—and though it is a source of intense pain, its energy comes from continual creative motion. . . .[24]

The diverse identity of all Latinas ultimately finds its unity in creativity. The Mexican-American woman from Chicago or Los Angeles or El Paso or San Antonio; the Dominican-American; the Cuban-American; the Puerto Rican-American; the Brazilian-American; the Jewish Chilean-American—they have learned to juggle cultures, perpetually living on the border of one reality and another, but ever able to reach deep inside themselves to create literature that illuminates for us all their individual experiences as Latinas, their personal cultural depths, and the multicultural pluralistic reality that is the America we inhabit.

We have entitled this anthology "Daughters of the Fifth Sun," a phrase reminiscent of the Spanish *hijos del quinto sol,* meaning children of the present age. One sacred belief of the Aztec, the Maya, the Quiché, and other indigenous peoples of the Americas, ancient and modern, is that the universe has known five ages. The present age is known as the Fifth Sun, *Quinto Sol.* "In this age," asked Cuahtencoztli, an ancient Aztec philosopher, "how is truth best spoken?" He was answered by Prince Tecayehuatzin, who said that only "flower-and-song," *floricanto,* can express truth. *Daughters of the Fifth Sun* is a *floricanto* offering—the truth of the Latina experience as it is best expressed in fiction and in poetry.

–Bryce Milligan
Mary Guerrero Milligan
Angela de Hoyos
San Antonio, Tejas, 1995

Notes

1. The term "Latina" has become the preferred term among writers and critics in the U.S., allowing as it does for multiple countries of origin. "Latina" and "Latino" are gender specific terms, with both genders being indicated by the admittedly awkward "Latino/a" or "Latina/Latino." By historical association, the term "Chicano" can still include both genders when it refers to individuals or groups active during the *movimiento Chicano* (approximately 1965 to 1980). "Chicana" came into common usage when the politicization of the U.S. women's movement became confluent with that of the *movimiento*. "Chicano" and "Chicana" are still the terms favored by some writers, though these terms technically refer only to persons of Mexican or southwestern U.S. origin. While the term "Mexican-American" is still current, it is objectionable to many on the grounds that it implies second-class citizenship. "Hispanic," by virtue of its governmental usage and its apparent inclusiveness, is used by a few writers and critics, but most find the term objectionable since it refers (technically) only to individuals of Spanish extraction. On the other hand, "Hispana" is used by scholars of the colonial period, especially in California and New Mexico, where class distinctions between pure blood and mixed blood were maintained. The term "mestiza," indicating specifically a mixture of Spanish and indigenous blood,

has both scholarly and popular usage. "Latino/Latina" has the advantage of referring to a common linguistic base, that is, Spanish, rather than to a specific ethnicity. Other terms in common usage include "Tejana," "Californiana," and "Mexicana," which refer to Latinas with roots or residency in various geographic regions.

2. See the important "Anthology No. 1," *Essays on la mujer,* eds. Rosaura Sánchez and Rosa Martínez Cruz (Los Angeles: UCLA/Chicano Studies Center Publications, 1977). The breadth of topics addressed in this anthology—from "Participación de las mujeres en la sociedad prehispánica" to "The Chicana Labor Force" to "The Role of the Chicana Within the Student Movement"—indicates the sort of scholarly explosion that occurred at this time.

3. María Herrera-Sobek, ed. *Beyond Stereotypes: The Critical Analysis of Chicana Literature* (Binghamton: Bilingual Press, 1985), p. 17.

4. See Marta Cotera's *Diosa y Hembra: The History and Heritage of Chicanas in the U.S.* (Austin: Information Systems, 1976) for a more extensive history. See also her *Profile of the Mexican American Woman* (Austin: National Education Laboratory, 1976). The best published source on Nuevo-mexicanas to date is *Nuestras Mujeres: Hispanas of New Mexico, Their Images and Their Lives, 1582–1992,* edited by Tey Diana Rebolledo, Erlinda Gonzáles-Berry, and Millie Santillanes (Albuquerque: El Norte Publications, 1992).

5. Antonia I. Castañeda, "Memory, Language, and Voice of Mestiza Women on the Northern Frontier: Historical Documents as Literary Texts," in *Recovering the U.S. Hispanic Literary Heritage,* ed. Ramón Gutiérrez and Genaro Padilla (Houston: Arte Público Press, 1993), p. 265.

6. A new critical edition of María Amparo Ruíz de Burton's *The Squatter and the Don,* edited by Rosaura Sánchez and Beatrice Pita, was published as part of the "Recovering the U.S. Hispanic Literary Heritage" series by Arte Público Press

in 1993. Sánchez and Pita are completing work on Ruiz de Burton's novel *Who Would Have Thought It?*

An edited translation of one of the Bancroft narratives, by Doña Eulalia Pérez, was included in *Infinite Divisions: An Anthology of Chicana Literature*, edited by Tey Diana Rebolledo and Eliana S. Rivero (Tucson: University of Arizona Press, 1993).

7. Carolyn Ashbaugh, *Lucy Parsons: American Revolutionary* (Chicago: Charles Herr for the Illinois Labor History Society, 1976). Albert and Lucy Parsons were extremely close, and Lucy's *Life of Albert R. Parsons, with Brief History of the Labor Movement in America* (Chicago: self-published, 1903) contains much information on the author's life and views as well as the life and views of her subject.

8. Alfredo Mirandé and Evangelina Enríquez, *La Chicana: The Mexican-American Woman* (Chicago: University of Chicago Press, 1979), p. 95.

9. Marian Arkin and Barbara Shollar, eds. *Longman Anthology of World Literature by Women, 1875–1975* (New York: Longman, 1989), pp. 199–202. It should be noted that of the nearly three hundred women writers from over fifty countries selected by the editors for inclusion in this major anthology, the four women with Texas connections represented are all Hispanic— Leonor Villegas de Magnón, Sara Estela Ramírez, Angela de Hoyos and Inés Hernández. See also Clara Lomas, "Mexican Precursors of Chicana Feminist Writing," in *Multiethnic Literature of the United States,* ed. Cordelia Candelaria (Boulder: University of Colorado at Boulder, 1989), pp. 21–33.

10. Inés Hernández, "Sara Estela Ramírez: The Early Twentieth Century Texas-Mexican Poet" (University of Houston, unpublished dissertation, 1984), p. 112.

11. Juanita Luna Lawhn, "El Regidor and La Prensa: Impediments to Women's Self-Definition," in *Third Woman,* IV: 1989, pp. 134–142.

12. Juanita Luna Lawhn, "Feminism in *La Prensa:* Women's Response to the Ideology of *El México de Afuera,"*

paper delivered at the University of Texas at Arlington; and "The Generation of *El México de Afuera* in San Antonio, Texas," also unpublished, which introduces a bibliography of Hispanic San Antonio publications. Both papers are part of Lawhn's on-going research into Hispanic Texas-Mexican women writers and are subject to periodic updates; on file in the library of San Antonio College.

13. See note 11. These conclusions are based on numerous interviews conducted over Bryce Milligan's ten years as book critic for the *San Antonio Express* and the *San Antonio Light,* as well as from published interviews conducted by other critics.

14. Jovita González, "Among My People," in *Tone the Bell Easy,* ed. J. Frank Dobie (Austin: Publications of the Texas Folklore Society, 1932). E. E. Mireles, R. B. Fisher, and Jovita G. Mireles, *Mi Libro Español* (Austin: Benson Co., 1941). Jovita González de Mireles, "The Guadalupana Vine," in *Texas Folk and Folklore,* ed. Mody Boatright, et al. (Dallas: Publications of the Texas Folklore Society, 1954). Jovita Gonzáles (*sic*) de Mireles, "After the Barbed Wire Came Hunger," in *Aztlán: An Anthology of Mexican American Literature,* edited by Stan Steiner (New York: Knopf, 1972). Charles Tatum, ed. *Mexican American Literature* (San Diego: Harcourt Brace Jovanovich, 1990), pp. 225–233.

15. Raymond Parades, "The Evolution of Chicano Literature," in *Three American Literatures,* ed. Houston A. Baker (New York: Modern Language Association, 1982), pp. 33–79.

16. Juan Bruce-Novoa, *Retrospace: Collected Essays on Chicano Literature* (Houston: Arte Público, 1990). See pages 132–145 for an excellent discussion of the canonical and non-canonical texts of Chicano literature.

17. Carmen Salazar Parr and Genevieve M. Ramírez, "The Female Hero in Chicano Literature," in *Beyond Stereotypes,* op. cit., pp. 47–59.

18. Op. cit., pp. 153–164.

19. See *Current Biography 1949,* pp. 455–456. Also Amy

• Notes •

Freeman Lee, "Playmaker of Mexico," *San Antonio Express News,* 4 June 1939, and "Josephina [*sic*] Niggli" in *The Carolina Playmakers: The First 50 Years* (Chapel Hill: University of North Carolina Press, 1970). Obituary (by John Igo) in *North San Antonio Times,* 22 December 1983.

20. Josefina Niggli, "Call Them Dreams," in *Pax: A Journal for Peace through Culture,* III, nos. 1–2 (San Antonio: 1985–1986), pp. 98–102.

21. Estela Portillo, "Introduction," in *El Grito* (Berkeley: Quinto Sol Publications, 1973), p. 5.

22. Evangelina Vigil, ed. "Woman of Her Word: Hispanic Women Write," special issue of *Revista Chicano-Riqueña* XI, 3–4 (1983), p. 7.

23. Cherríe Moraga, "Introduction," in *This Bridge Called My Back: Writings by Radical Women of Color,* edited by Cherríe Moraga and Gloria Anzaldúa, second edition (Latham, NY: Kitchen Table: Women of Color Press, 1983), p. (iii).

24. Gloria Anzaldúa, *Borderlands/La Frontera: The New Mestiza* (Spinsters/Aunt Lute Books, 1987), pp. 79–80.

A Note on Italics

Traditional usage requires that languages other than English in a predominantly English text be set in italics. Some of the authors in this anthology still adhere to this practice in their fiction and poetry. Others have adopted a different position. The bilingual idiom has become in some parts of this country a language unto itself, with both Spanish and English bearing equal weight. In this context, some authors have dropped the standard italic usage. This anthology respects the different style each author prefers to use in her work.

DENISE CHÁVEZ

The Wedding

IF MY MARRIAGE is going to be like my wed - ding, then I'm in for a lot of trouble. For one thing, that Saturday there was a tornado watch all day. We never have tornadoes in Agua Oscura. I don't know anyone that's ever seen one either. I can't ask any relatives about it. I don't have any. I didn't even ask my stepbrothers and stepsisters to the wedding, not that they would have come. I don't like them. Now my stepmom, Lucha, she woulda come. My stepdad, Arturo, he mighta come too, except they're both dead. I guess family not being there means they won't get in the way. Not *my* family, anyway. Hector's family might. His mom, Dolly, likes to get in the middle of things, and so does his sister, Soveida. They always have to know what you're doing. They'll settle down. It's the old lady, Lupita, who really worries me. She told me when we were alone that if it weren't for me, Hector could have a future. I told Hector, and he said: "Relax, Mamá's old. She doesn't like that you're pregnant."

"Well, that's just too bad. I am and there's nothing she can do about it, Hector."

"Just relax, babes, she'll chill."

I don't know, she's pretty scary in that way old ladies who don't like you can be scary. And yet, I like her. If I had a grandmother, I'd probably want one just like her. She's kinda short, with a little extra padding so that she hugs solid the way only a woman like that can. I don't know, maybe Mamá will like me someday. Maybe when the baby is born.

But I was telling you about the wedding. When I woke up this morning it was already ten o'clock, and I hadn't done my hair yet. By the time I put in the rinse and curled it, it was noon. I woke up late, because I'd gone out with La Virgie Lozano and some other girlfriends the night before. We drove to El Paso to see a male revue, the Chippendales. They weren't so Chippendale, after all. One of the guys had real skinny legs and another was too hairy. "These aren't no Chippendales," I told La Virgie, "the Chippendales don't have no body hair. Someone messed up. These guys are from Ysleta or Sunland Park. Somebody just handed them a jock strap and forgot to grease them up."

I took a long time with my hair and then I had to do my nails. I wanted to be sure all the little gold wedding bells were glued on tight on all my fingernails. That took me until one. The wedding was at two o'clock. I was barely in my dress when El Gonie and La Virgie came to get me to take me to the church. I wasn't supposed to see Hector before the wedding. Now that's pretty hard when you're living in the same apartment.

So he spent the night at his mom's. El Gonie says they went out drinking. As for me, I slept the best I've slept in a long time. Not enough. But really good.

Hector promised me he'd have the rings there and to tell you the truth, I was worried. When I walked down the aisle, I didn't know if the rings were going to be there or not. If they weren't, I was gonna kill him.

"You'll have to wait and see them," he said.

"I don't want no Woolworth rings, Hector Dosamantes, you hear me? Nothing cheap with gold that chips off the first sinkful of dishes. Which by the way, we're gonna share. If you expect me to be your slave, you have another thing in your brain. We're gonna share the housework, not like how it's been, me cleaning up after you like I was your mother or something. When we're married, things are going to change."

"Oh yeah?" Hector says. "I suppose you'll lose your interest in sex. That's what El Gonie said happened after his first and second marriages. Soon as they had the papers, Nora Jean and Tancy lost interest. No way I'll support that, Ada," he tells me.

And I tell him: "Don't worry about it so much. I'm pregnant, aren't I? I showed an interest before, so just don't think about it now."

"I got to think about it. That's what marriage is: sexual relations, two bodies melting into one."

"Oh yeah?" I says. "Well, it's even more than that. It's holding hands and having a family and taking care of each other. I've never had a family of my own, so now I want one."

"Why do you think I'm getting married? To have a son."

"Do we have to call the baby Hector Jr.? That's the stupidest, dumbest name in the whole world."

"It's *my* name."

"That's what I mean."

"Well, if it's a boy we have to call him Hector, Jr."

"And if it's a girl?"

"If it's a girl, which it won't be, I'll figure it out."

I'm hoping the baby's a girl. If it's a boy, well, no way he's going to be called Hector, Jr.

So here I am walking up the aisle, by myself, no one to walk me up. When I get to the front, I trip over Mr. Dosamantes' lap robe. He's in a wheelchair sitting up there on the groom's side, but his blanket is over on the bride's side of the pews. This is Our Lady of Grace Church. The grandmother's idea. I wanted to say our vows in Juárez and spend the night over there at Sylvia's listening to mariachis, but no way.

I nearly trip and I drag the blanket with me as Hector pulls it back. Then El Gonie picks it up. Soveida is out of her pew, and Lupita's maid starts giggling. I get mad, but then Hector looks at me, and I say *Jesus, just settle down,* with my eyes, and I walk up to the altar. The priest is up there. I don't like the way he looks. All skinny and like he's about to tell you how holy he is. He's Filipino or something, and the guy doesn't have a sense of humor. And what's even worse, the priest keeps forgetting my name.

"Do you . . . ah . . . ah . . . take Hector for your lawful, wedded, husband . . . Hector, do you take . . . ah . . . ah . . . ah . . . as your . . . ah . . . lawful wedded wife?"

"Ada," I say. "A-d-a." The priest can't remember my name, and we have to pay him for the honor of marrying us! Then. Out comes this ring that looks like it came out of a Cracker Jack box. I don't like it, but I put the damn thing on anyway, only it doesn't fit. It's too tight. Which reminds me of the saying: The way you get married shows how your life together as man and wife is going to be. A tight fit, I think.

I can barely get the ring on, but I finally do, and then it's time for the I do's.

I can hardly hear Hector, he sounds like he's about thirteen years old. We "I do" at the same time, and then we laugh and then we "I do" again at the same time. Everyone in the church starts laughing, and I get embarrassed. Then Hector forgets to lift up the veil when he goes to kiss me. More laughter. La Virgie steps in to lift it up, and Hector misses my mouth, so I grab him and cheers break out. Now he's embarrassed and we walk down the aisle: man, wife, and baby. Mr. Dosamantes' wheelchair is finally out of the way. Everyone stands up and we go outside where they throw birdseed.

"Birdseed? What happened to the rice, Soveida? I always wanted rice!"

"Rice isn't good for the birds, Ada. They say it's better to have birdseed. The birds choke on the rice."

"Shit! This is my wedding and I wanted rice."

"Forget it babes, we're having rice at the reception," says Hector.

"That's Spanish rice, Hector, not the kind of rice I'm talking about. I wanted Uncle Ben's converted rice."

"Sorry, Ada," says Soveida.

And I say, "Whose damn wedding is this, anyway?"

After we got outside, I noticed the wind had come up. I forgot about the tornado watch. The sky did look a little darker, this was about three o'clock, but it still seemed all right. After kissing and hugging ten thousand of Hector's relatives I didn't know, we went to Rogelio's Fine Photography to take pictures. The wedding party was there, which was me and Hector, the Best Man, El Gonie, and the Maid of Honor, La Virgie. Everyone got mad at me for picking her as Maid of Honor. (Dolly, Soveida, and the old grandma did, anyway.) But like I say, whose wedding is this? Everybody seems to keep forgetting.

La Virgie's no Maid of Honor. She's got five kids and no husband, but she's my friend. Or she was my friend. I didn't know her too good, but Hector and I used to go out with her and El Gonie a lot. The Maid of Honor was between her and Soveida. I probably shoulda picked Soveida. La Virgie was the reason Soveida got divorced from her first husband. Oh well. If I'd known what was going to happen at the reception, I never woulda picked La Virgie Lozano as my Maid of Honor. She doesn't have no Honor. And she's certainly no Maid. She's a tramp, but I didn't know that until about ten p.m. that night in the parking lot of the Knights of Columbus Hall.

Just ask me what could go wrong at the wedding reception, and I'll tell you nothing went right; although for all the things that went wrong, one thing did go right. But I'll tell you about that later. First off, we get into the Knights of Columbus Hall and I notice there's litter all over the outside. Turns out the janitor didn't clean up like he was supposed to. There's bingo cards all over the folding tables. Hector groans when he sees his cousin, M.J., at the guest book. He never liked her. I'm not exactly sure yet why he hates most of his relatives. I'll have time to find that out after the wedding. What I really want to know about is his cousin Mara, the one everyone always talks about in a whisper. Soveida invited her to the wedding, but she decided not to come.

"Shit!" Hector whispers loudly. "Tía Adelaida's serving punch." I turn to look at this half-man half-woman serving the sherbert punch. I never wanted sherbert punch, but what can you do? The bride is the last person to know anything.

"Who is she?" I say.

"Mi tía Adelaida. My mom's aunt. She's been paralyzed for fifty years."

"Speaking of paralyzed," I said, "who brought your dad to the church?"

"My mom and her boyfriend, Reldon! Can you believe that!"

"That's nice."

"Nice! What are you, crazy? My grandmother isn't speaking to my mom now."

"Who's that waving to you, Hector?"

"Shit! It's A.J. My first cousin. He's a fag."

"He wants to take a picture. Smile."

"Up his ass! Or maybe I should say up his nose!"

Things went from okay to not so okay to kinda strange to really awful to the real bitching pits.

Of course, Hector got drunk, but not before El Gonie, who was serving champagne and who brought several kegs of beer at the last moment.

Mr. Dosamantes even got drunk! They say that paralyzed people get drunk faster than normal people. He's not really totally paralyzed, just kinda drooly and saggy on the left side. Soveida says he should get better. Someone left Mr. D. in his wheelchair next to the champagne punch, and he kept refilling his little paper cup from the little spouty fountains that came out of the side and splashed on the dry ice. Dolly got mad at him; they had a fight, but her boyfriend, Reldon, broke it up. They were fighting about him getting drunk and then asking Mamá

Lupita's maid, Tere, to take him to the bathroom. Dolly got mad at that because she said he shouldn't be asking no pretty young girls to take him to the bathroom. And he started screaming at her that fine, he would just wet his pants then and there. *"I'll* take you to the bathroom," Dolly says. And Mr. D. says, "No way, we're divorced."

Reldon didn't seem to like that idea anyway, and so he volunteers to take Mr. D. to pee. The rest of the night Lupita starts to like Reldon. Which makes Mr. D. pissed. So Mr. D. starts in fighting with his ex-Mrs. D. And she yells at him about how she doesn't like the way he looks at Tere; and he says, "Well look at the way your son is looking at her and she's looking at him." But that makes Dolly even madder. And it even starts to bother me. Everyone is drunk by now. Mr. D. is fighting with his ex-Mrs. D., but we forgot about them when El Gonie and La Virgie started dancing all sexy on the dance floor like they were going to make love out there.

About that time Lupita stepped up to the microphone and introduced tío somebody, who read a long poem in Spanish that he said he composed for the wedding. Then someone named El Bluey—it turned out to be Hector's *tío* Bluey, his *tía* Pina's husband—led the wedding marcha around the room. That was the fun part of the wedding. All night people kept pinning dollar bills on my dress. Each dollar bill gives you a chance to dance with either the bride or the groom. My dress was full of pins and dollar bills and so was Hector's suit.

Suddenly, after the marcha I started feeling queasy so I went to the bathroom. A bunch of teenage girls were in there smoking, and the smell got me to feeling worse. I'd eaten the tamales, the macaroni salad, the beans and chile, and the jello salad already, and I'd had at least five champagnes and two beers. I don't know if it was the jumping around during the marcha, going under the London bridge with my head all bent down, snaking around the room with the little hop, or the baby, but I threw up in there for awhile. When I came out, I couldn't find Hector. Neither could Soveida nor anyone else. I danced with a viejito, somebody from Rincón, who had bad breath, which made me queasy again. That made me go back into the bathroom where the girls were still smoking. When I came out, I decided to go outside and get some fresh air and to see if the tornado was coming our way after all.

That's when I got the surprise I wasn't expecting. The wind had picked up. With the parking lot lights I could see the open door of Hector's Bonneville, which La Virgie decorated with pink and blue Kleenex flowers. I decided to go over there to close the door. Who do I see inside but La Virgie, her Maid-of-Honor top down to her waist, and there's Hector inside the back seat sucking on one of her chi chis. Well, I got sick all over Hector's tux legs, but not before I pulled him out of the back seat and hit him like I never hit anybody before in my life. He kept saying, "Babes, Baby, baby, babes . . ." the way he does, and I let him have it good in between babes. I was yelling and screaming and El Gonie and Soveida came out. El Gonie took that puta home, and I said, "I never want to see you again, you slut. I shoulda picked Soveida as my Maid of Honor!" And you know what the little puta bitch did? She laughed her little puta bitch laugh. And then she walked off like she had espinas, little stickers up her little puta bitch ass.

Soveida pulled me back into the car and settled me down. Not that many people knew what had gone on. Not that night anyway. Soveida didn't want her mother or grandmother to know. I said they should know their little baby boy is a pinche cabrón. And Soveida said, I think they already know that. I stopped screaming and went back inside to the bathroom with Soveida. I had had it. I started screaming at the teenagers: "Get the hell out of here you little shits, go smoke outside!" Whose wedding is this, anyway? All that smoke was giving me the asco bad. I stayed in the bathroom for a good half hour sitting on top of a toilet with my dress all bunched up on my lap. Finally Hector comes in, scaring an old lady who was pulling down her slip, and I start yelling again.

Finally the pendejo convinced me that we'd talk about it later at the Motel 6. We'd planned on staying at the Hilton or maybe La Quinta, but there was a poodle convention in town and there weren't many rooms left.

"This is a wedding, Ada, not a funeral. No one wants to see us fighting."

"I'm not convinced, Hector. You've twisted around my head, I'm not sure any more."

Soveida came in and said that I could figure everything out tomorrow and that she supported me and I could move in with her until I figured out what I wanted to do. Then a gigantic light bulb exploded in my head and I said, "I'm married and I'm going to have a baby!"

I started crying; Hector started crying and said:

"We won't call him Hector Jr., Ada, if that's what you want. We'll call him whatever you want, babes."

"I can? Do you mean that, Hector?"

That kind of softened me up, and he promised he'd never see La Virgie ever again, that she was out of his life, and that it was her fault, the whole thing. He explained it to me:

"When you went to the bathroom, La Virgie pinned a five-dollar bill near my cómo se llama and said dance with me. The band played "Leila," and after that we were both so hot from dancing that she suggested we go outside to get some fresh air. I decided to get a pack of cigarettes from the glove compartment. I opened up the car and that's when she got in. Suddenly she unzipped her top and there she was in a strapless bra that she pulled down. I yelled to her that someone might see her. When I got in the back seat to cover her up with my tux jacket, she shoved her nipple in my face."

"So why was she saying in a soft voice, put it in, put it in . . ."

"She meant the nipple. A la V, Ada!"

"Oh yeah? Well, I'm not so sure. Don't you a la V me!"

We went around and around until Soveida says, "You two get out of this bathroom. People are asking about you. Someone is giving you a toast."

I hugged Soveida and said, "Thank you, girl." I knew it was hard for her seeing Ivan there with his latest girlfriend. And she says, "I'm healed." Hector invited him. Not me. Even though Soveida says she's recovered from the man, I still feel she loves him the way you love red chile even though it burns you up inside and gives you the hot runs.

Finally I said what the hell and came out of the bathroom with Hector. The band was playing a sweetheart tune and everyone sees us and starts cheering. The *tía* with the mustache grabs my arm. She's got a grip like a truck driver. She starts crying and says "¡Que Díos los bendiga!"

Yeah, sure. But we dance like nothing is wrong, and I keep softening toward the cabrón each circle around the damn K of C Hall.

He grabs me close and whispers: "Let's go, babes!"

"Don't you babes me no more, cabrón! I'll go with you, but tomorrow I'm filing for divorce."

We smile at his primo the fag and at the *tía* with the strong arms and the mustache, who waves to me across the room still crying, and then we get our things as everyone starts cheering again and whispering and laughing and El Gonie jabs Hector and smiles dirty and then starts up with: "I know what you're going to do."

"Don't count on it, Gonie," I say.

We leave the K of C Hall and drive to the Motel 6. I turn on the television and watch some commercial for something that gets rid of acne. I get so bored I go through Hector's wallet and get his MasterCard and order two tubes of the acne creme. Hector's a long time in the bathroom. Good. Stay there. But he comes out naked and smelling of Canoe aftershave and I just turn up the volume on the TV.

"Aren't you going to give me my rights?"

"Suffer, babes," I said. "You already had your rights and your wrongs. I don't want to talk about it now. I need to think about everything. So leave me alone."

Hector falls asleep on the other double bed in the room, and I stay up to watch "The Bug." I don't get the ending when the scientist goes crazy. He falls into the big pit as the fire bugs get in his hair and burn his clothing. I don't get what happened, but then I missed the beginning. What was really cool was when the bugs spelled out the guys name on the wall. Maybe if there's cucarachas here they'll come out in the middle of the night and spell

out something for me. D-I-V-O-R-C-E. I try to forget it's
my wedding night.

I wake up real early with Hector in the bed with me
and he's warm and I lay there until I can't stand it no
longer as he moves closer and says to me the usual: "Come
on babes, come on."

I melt like he knows I will and we make love, except
I won't turn around to look at him. It's okay this way and
he holds me and rocks me back and forth and I cry to my-
self, and I think: I'm married. I'm really married. And
I'm having a baby. Then the bug movie flashes to me, and
I think I see the words *STUPID PENDEJA* on the wall.

The one good thing that came out of the whole stupid thing is that now I don't have to call the baby Hector
Jr. if I don't want. I never liked kids called Ray Jr., or Sal
Jr., or Ben Jr. Let the kid be himself, I think. I really do
hope the baby is a girl. If it is, then I will call her Nereid.
The name of some kind of spirit that I read about in junior high English class. Nereids were these beautiful spirits. The name just kind of stuck with me all these years.
Just let Hector try and change my mind about this.

That's if the baby's a girl.

If the baby's a boy, I'm going to call him Michael
John. I'm not calling him that for Hector or for nobody.
I'm calling him that just for me. The way I call myself
Ada. Not Narada. Not Nada. Ada.

PAT MORA

Uncoiling

With thorns, she scratches
 on my window, tosses her hair dark with rain,
  snares lightning, cholla, hawks, butterfly
   swarms in the tangles.

She sighs clouds,
 head thrown back, eyes closed, roars
                              and rivers leap,
boulders retreat like crabs
into themselves.

She spews gusts and thunder,
 spooks pale women who scurry to
  lock doors, windows
   when her tumbleweed skirt starts its spin.

They sing lace lullabies
    so their children won't hear
        her uncoiling
           through her lips, howling
               leaves off trees, flesh
                   off bones, until she becomes

sound, spins herself
    to sleep, sand stinging her ankles,
        whirring into her raw skin like stars.

MIRIAM BORNSTEIN

On
Becoming
Round

Like Neruda
I tried to write this poem
with green ink
—it is not a literary stand
but a way of understanding.

However, Neruda never knew about pots and pans
and putting words in little hands.
He looked at the sea,
      contemplated the origin of rocks
            imprisoned ships in imaginary bottles
                  and looked at shells *como mujeres*
                  como Matilde
                  whose hand smoothed his hair
                        against the cold wind.

He, too, became round
more out of old age
than out of life.

It is easier to become round by the sea.

Nada

Almost as soon as Doña Ernestina got the telegram about her son's having been killed in Vietnam, she started giving her possessions away. At first we didn't realize what she was doing. By the time we did, it was too late.

The army people had comforted Doña Ernestina with the news that her son's "remains" would have to be "collected and shipped" back to New Jersey at some later date, since other "personnel" had also been lost on the same day. In other words, she would have to wait until Tony's body could be processed.

Processed. Doña Ernestina spoke that word like a curse when she told us. We were all down in El Basement—that's what we called the cellar of our apartment building: no windows for light, boilers making such a racket that you could scream and almost no one would hear you. Some of us had started meeting here on Saturday mornings—as much to talk as to wash our clothes—and over the years it became a sort of women's club where we could catch up on a week's worth of gossip. That Saturday, however, I had dreaded going down the cement steps. All of us had just heard the news about Tony the night before.

I should have known the minute I saw her, holding court in her widow's costume, that something had cracked inside Doña Ernestina. She was in full *luto*—black from head to toe, including a mantilla. In contrast, Lydia and Isabelita were both in rollers and bathrobes: our customary uniform for these Saturday morning gatherings—maybe our way of saying "No Men Allowed." As I approached them, Lydia stared at me with a scared-rabbit look in her eyes.

Doña Ernestina simply waited for me to join the other two leaning against the machines before she continued explaining what had happened when the news of Tony had arrived at her door the day before. She spoke calmly, a haughty expression on her face, looking like an offended duchess in her beautiful black dress. She was pale, pale, but she had a wild look in her eyes. The officer had told her that—when the time came—they would bury Tony with "full military honors"; for now they were sending her the medal and a flag. But she had said, *"No, gracias,"* to the funeral, and she sent the flag and medals back marked *Ya no vive aquí:* Does not live here anymore. "Tell the Mr. President of the United States what I say: *No, gracias."* Then she waited for our response.

Lydia shook her head, indicating that she was speechless. And Elenita looked pointedly at me, forcing me to be the one to speak the words of sympathy for all of us, to reassure Doña Ernestina that she had done exactly what any of us would have done in her place: yes, we would have all said *No, gracias,* to any president who had actually tried to pay for a son's life with a few trinkets and a folded flag.

Doña Ernestina nodded gravely. Then she picked up the stack of neatly folded men's shirts from the sofa (a discard we had salvaged from the sidewalk) and walked regally out of El Basement.

Lydia, who had gone to high school with Tony, burst into tears as soon as Doña Ernestina was out of sight. Elenita and I sat her down between us on the sofa and held her until she had let most of it out. Lydia is still young—a woman who has not yet been visited too often by *la muerte*. Her husband of six months has just gotten his draft notice, and they have been trying for a baby—trying very hard. The walls of El Building are thin enough so that it has become a secret joke (kept only from Lydia and Roberto) that he is far more likely to escape the draft due to acute exhaustion than by becoming a father.

"Doesn't Doña Ernestina feel *anything?*" Lydia asked in between sobs. "Did you see her, dressed up like an actress in a play—and not one tear for her son?"

"We all have different ways of grieving," I said, though I couldn't help thinking that there *was* a strangeness to Doña Ernestina and that Lydia was right when she said that the woman seemed to be acting out a part. "I think we should wait and see what she is going to do."

"Maybe," said Elenita. "Did you get a visit from *el padre* yesterday?"

We nodded, not surprised to learn that all of us had gotten personal calls from Padre Alvaro, our painfully shy priest, after Doña Ernestina had frightened him away. Apparently *el padre* had come to her apartment immediately after hearing about Tony, expecting to comfort the woman as he had when Don Antonio died suddenly a year ago. Her grief then had been understandable in its immensity, for she had been burying not only her husband but also the dream shared by many of the barrio women her age—that of returning with her man to the Island after retirement, of buying a *casita* in the old pueblo, and of being buried on native ground alongside *la familia.* People *my* age—those of us born or raised here—have had our mothers drill this fantasy into our brains all of our lives. So when Don Antonio dropped his head on the domino table, scattering the ivory pieces of the best game of the year, and when he was laid out in his best black suit at Ramírez's Funeral Home, all of us knew how to talk to the grieving widow.

That was the last time we saw both her men. Tony was there, too—home on a two-day pass from basic training—and he cried like a little boy over his father's handsome face, calling him Papi, Papi. Doña Ernestina had had a full mother's duty then, taking care of the hysterical boy. It was a normal chain of grief, the strongest taking care of the weakest. We buried Don Antonio at Garden State Memorial Park, where there are probably more Puerto Ricans than on the Island. Padre Alvaro said his sermon in a soft, trembling voice that was barely audible over the cries of the boy being supported on one side by his mother, impressive in her quiet strength and dignity, and on the other by Cheo, owner of the bodega where Don Antonio had played dominoes with other barrio men of his age for over twenty years.

Just about everyone from El Building had attended that funeral, and it had been done right. Doña Ernestina had sent her son off to fight for America and then had started collecting her widow's pension. Some of us asked Doña Iris (who knew how to read cards) about Doña Ernestina's future, and Doña Iris had said: "A long journey within a year"—which fit with what we had thought would happen next: Doña Ernestina would move back to the Island and wait with her relatives for Tony to come home from the war. Some older women actually went home when they started collecting social security or pensions, but that was rare. Usually, it seemed to me, somebody had to die before the island dream would come true for women like Doña Ernestina. As for my friends and me, we talked about "vacations" in the Caribbean. But we knew that if life was hard for us in this barrio, it would be worse in a pueblo where no one knew us (and had maybe only heard of our parents before they came to *Los Estados Unidos de América,* where most of us had been brought as children).

When Padre Alvaro had knocked softly on my door, I had yanked it open, thinking it was that ex-husband of mine asking for a second chance again. (That's just the way Miguel knocks when he's sorry for leaving me— about once a week—when he wants a loan.) So I was wearing my go-to-hell face when I threw open the door, and the poor priest nearly jumped out of his skin. I saw him take a couple of deep breaths before he asked me in his slow way—he tries to hide his stutter by dragging out his words—if I knew whether or not Doña Ernestina was ill. After I said, "No, not that I know," Padre Alvaro just stood there, looking pitiful, until I asked him if he cared to come in. I had been sleeping on the sofa and watching TV all afternoon, and I really didn't want him to see the mess, but I had nothing to fear. The poor man actually took one step back at my invitation. No, he was in a hurry, he had a few other parishioners to visit, etc. These were difficult times, he said, so-so-so many young people lost to drugs or dying in the wa-wa-war. I asked him if *he* thought Doña Ernestina was sick, but he just shook his head. The man looked like an orphan at my door with those sad, brown eyes. He was actually appealing in a homely way; that long nose nearly touched the tip of his chin when he smiled, and his big crooked teeth broke my heart.

"She does not want to speak to me," Padre Alvaro said as he caressed a large silver crucifix that hung on a thick chain around his neck. He seemed to be dragged down by its weight, stoop-shouldered and skinny as he was.

I felt a strong impulse to feed him some of my chicken soup, still warm on the stove from my supper. Contrary to what Lydia says about me behind my back, I like living by myself. And I could not have been happier to have that mama's boy Miguel back where he belonged—with his mother, who thought that he was still her baby. But this scraggly thing at my door needed home cooking and maybe even something more than a hot meal to bring a little spark into his life. (I mentally asked God to forgive me for having thoughts like these about one of his priests. Ay *bendito,* but they too are made of flesh and blood.)

"Maybe she just needs a little more time, Padre," I said in as comforting a voice as I could manage. Unlike the other women in El Building, I am not convinced that priests are truly necessary—or even much help—in times of crisis.

"Sí, hija, perhaps you're right," he muttered sadly—calling me "daughter" even though I'm pretty sure I'm five or six years older. (Padre Alvaro seems so "untouched" that it's hard to tell his age. I mean, when you live, it shows. He looks hungry for love, starving himself by choice.) I promised him that I would look in on Doña Ernestina. Without another word, he made the sign of the cross in the air between us and turned away. As I heard his slow steps descending the creaky stairs, I asked myself: What do priests dream about?

When *el padre*'s name came up again during that Saturday meeting in El Basement, I asked my friends what *they* thought a priest dreamed about. It was a fertile subject, so much so that we spent the rest of our laundry time coming up with scenarios. Before the last drier stopped, we all agreed that we could not receive communion the next day at mass unless we went to confession that afternoon and told another priest, not Alvaro, about our "unclean thoughts."

As for Doña Ernestina's situation, we agreed that we should be there for her if she called, but the decent thing to do, we decided, was to give her a little more time alone. Lydia kept repeating, in that childish way of hers, "Something is wrong with the woman," but she didn't volunteer to go see what it was that was making Doña Ernestina act so strangely. Instead she complained that she and Roberto had heard pots and pans banging and things being moved around for hours in 4-D last night— they had hardly been able to sleep. Isabelita winked at me behind Lydia's back. Lydia and Roberto still had not caught on: if they could hear what was going on in 4-D, the rest of us could also get an earful of what went on in 4-A. They were just kids who thought they had invented sex: I tell you, a *telenovela* could be made from the stories in El Building.

On Sunday Doña Ernestina was not at the Spanish mass, and I avoided Padre Alvaro so he would not ask me about her. But I was worried. Doña Ernestina was a church *cucaracha*—a devout Catholic who, like many of us, did not always do what the priests and the Pope or-

dered but who knew where God lived. Only a serious illness or tragedy could keep her from attending mass, so afterward I went straight to her apartment and knocked on
her door. There was no answer, although I had heard
scraping and dragging noises, like furniture being moved
around. At least she was on her feet and active. Maybe
housework was what she needed to snap out of her shock.
I decided to try again the next day.

As I went by Lydia's apartment, the young woman
opened her door—I knew she had been watching me
through the peephole—to tell me about more noises from
across the hall during the night. Lydia was in her baby-
doll pajamas. Although she stuck only her nose out, I
could see Roberto in his jockey underwear doing something in the kitchen. I couldn't help thinking about
Miguel and me when we had first gotten together. We
were an explosive combination. After a night of passionate lovemaking, I would walk around thinking: Do not
light cigarettes around me. No open flames. Highly combustible materials being transported. But when his mama
showed up at our door, the man of fire turned into a heap
of ashes at her feet.

"Let's wait and see what happens," I told Lydia again.

We did not have to wait for long. On Monday Doña
Ernestina called to invite us to a wake for Tony, a *velorio,*
in her apartment. The word spread fast. Everyone wanted
to do something for her. Cheo donated fresh chickens and
island produce of all kinds. Several of us got together and
made arroz con pollo, also flan for dessert. And Doña Iris
made two dozen *pasteles* and wrapped the meat pies in banana leaves that she had been saving in her freezer for her
famous Christmas parties. We women carried in our
steaming plates, while the men brought in their bottles

of Palo Viejo rum for themselves and candy-sweet Manischewitz wine for us. We came ready to spend the night saying our rosaries and praying for Tony's soul.

Doña Ernestina met us at the door and led us into her living room, where the lights were off. A photograph of Tony and one of her deceased husband Don Antonio were sitting on top of a table, surrounded by at least a dozen candles. It was a spooky sight that caused several of the older women to cross themselves. Doña Ernestina had arranged folding chairs in front of this table and told us to sit down. She did not ask us to take our food and drinks to the kitchen. She just looked at each of us individually, as if she were taking attendance in a class, and then said: "I have asked you here to say good-bye to my husband Antonio and my son Tony. You have been my friends and neighbors for twenty years, but they were my life. Now that they are gone, I have *nada. Nada. Nada.*"

I tell you, that word is like a drain that sucks everything down. Hearing her say *nada* over and over made me feel as if I were being yanked into a dark pit. I could feel the others getting nervous around me too, but here was a woman deep into her pain: we had to give her a little space. She looked around the room, then walked out without saying another word.

As we sat there in silence, stealing looks at each other, we began to hear the sounds of things being moved around in other rooms. One of the older women took charge then, and soon the drinks were poured, the food served—all this while the strange sounds kept coming from different rooms in the apartment. Nobody said much, except once when we heard something like a dish fall and break. Doña Iris pointed her index finger at her ear and made a couple of circles—and out of nervousness, I guess, some of us giggled like schoolchildren.

It was a long while before Doña Ernestina came back out to us. By then we were gathering our dishes and purses, having come to the conclusion that it was time to leave. Holding two huge Sears shopping bags, one in each hand, Doña Ernestina took her place at the front door as if she were a society hostess in a receiving line. Some of us women hung back to see what was going on. But Tito, the building's super, had had enough and tried to get past her. She took his hand, putting in it a small ceramic poodle with a gold chain around its neck. Tito gave the poodle a funny look, then glanced at Doña Ernestina as though he were scared and hurried away with the dog in his hand.

We were let out of her place one by one but not until she had forced one of her possessions on each of us. She grabbed without looking from her bags. Out came her prized *miniaturas,* knickknacks that take a woman a lifetime to collect. Out came ceramic and porcelain items of all kinds, including vases and ashtrays; out came kitchen utensils, dishes, forks, knives, spoons; out came old calendars and every small item that she had touched or been touched by in the last twenty years. Out came a bronzed baby shoe—and I got that.

As we left the apartment, Doña Iris said "Psst" to some of us, so we followed her down the hallway. "Doña Ernestina's faculties are temporarily out of order," she said very seriously. "It is due to the shock of her son's death."

We all said *Sí,* and nodded our heads.

"But what can we do?" Lydia said, her voice cracking

a little. "What should I do with this?" She was holding one of Tony's baseball trophies in her hand: 1968 Most Valuable Player, for the Pocos Locos, our barrio's team.

Doña Iris said, "Let us keep her things safe for her until she recovers her senses. And let her mourn in peace. These things take time. If she needs us, she will call us." Doña Iris shrugged her shoulders. *"Así es la vida, hijas:* That's the way life is."

As I passed Tito on the stairs, he shook his head while looking up at Doña Ernestina's door. "I say she needs a shrink. I think somebody should call the social worker." He did not look at me when he mumbled these things. By "somebody" he meant one of us women. He didn't want trouble in his building, and he expected one of us to get rid of the problems. I just ignored him.

In my bed I prayed to the Holy Mother that she would find peace for Doña Ernestina's troubled spirit, but things got worse. All that week Lydia saw strange things happening through the peephole on her door. Every time people came to Doña Ernestina's apartment—to deliver flowers or telegrams from the Island or anything—the woman would force something on them. She pleaded with them to take this or that; if they hesitated, she commanded them with those tragic eyes to accept a token of her life.

And they did, walking out of our apartment building, carrying cushions, lamps, doilies, clothing, shoes, umbrellas, wastebaskets, schoolbooks, and notebooks: things of value and things of no worth at all to anyone but the person who had owned them. Eventually winos and street people got the news of the great giveaway in 4-D, and soon there was a line down the stairs and out the door.

Nobody went home empty handed; it was like a soup kitchen. Lydia was afraid to step out of her place because of all the dangerous-looking characters hanging out on that floor. And the smell! Entering our building was like coming into a cheap bar and public urinal combined.

Isabelita, living alone with her two little children and fearing for their safety, was the one who finally called a meeting of the residents. Only the women attended, since the men were truly afraid of Doña Ernestina. It isn't unusual for men to be frightened when they see a woman go crazy. If they are not the cause of her madness, then they act as if they don't understand it and usually leave us alone to deal with our "woman's problems." This is just as well.

Maybe I *am* just bitter because of Miguel—I know what is said behind my back. But this is a fact: when a woman is in trouble, a man calls in her mama, her sisters, or her friends, and then he makes himself scarce until it's all over. This happens again and again. At how many bedsides of women have I sat? How many times have I made the doctor's appointment, taken care of the children, and fed the husbands of my friends in the barrio? It is not that the men can't do these things; it's just that they know how much women help each other. Maybe the men even suspect that we know one another better than they know their own wives. As I said, it is just as well that they stay out of our way when there is trouble. It makes things simpler for us.

At the meeting, Isabelita said right away that we should go up to 4-D and try to reason with *la pobre* Doña Ernestina. Maybe we could get her to give us a relative's address in Puerto Rico—the woman obviously needed to be taken care of. What she was doing was putting us all in a very difficult situation. There were no dissenters this time. We voted to go as a group to talk to Doña Ernestina the next morning.

But that night we were all awakened by crashing noises on the street. In the light of the full moon, I could see that the air was raining household goods: kitchen chairs, stools, a small TV, a nightstand, pieces of a bed frame. Everything was splintering as it landed on the pavement. People were running for cover and yelling up at our building. The problem, I knew instantly, was in apartment 4-D.

Putting on my bathrobe and slippers, I stepped out into the hall-way. Lydia and Roberto were rushing down the stairs, but on the flight above my landing, I caught up with Doña Iris and Isabelita, heading toward 4-D. Out of breath, we stood in the fourth-floor hall-way, listening to police sirens approaching our building in front. We could hear the slamming of car doors and yelling—in both Spanish and English. Then we tried the door to 4-D. It was unlocked.

We came into a room virtually empty. Even the pictures had been taken down from the walls; all that was left were the nail holes and the lighter places on the paint where the framed photographs had been for years. We took a few seconds to spot Doña Ernestina: she was curled up in the farthest corner of the living room, naked. *"Como salió a este mundo,"* said Doña Iris, crossing herself.

Just as she had come into the world. Wearing nothing. Nothing around her except a clean, empty room. *Nada.* She had left nothing behind—except the bottles of pills, the ones the doctors give to ease the pain, to numb you, to make you feel nothing when someone dies.

The bottles were empty too, and the policemen took them. But we didn't let them take Doña Ernestina until we each had brought up some of our own best clothes and dressed her like the decent woman that she was. *La decencia.* Nothing can ever change that—not even *la muerte.* This is the way life is. *Así es la vida.*

ROSEMARY CATACALOS

(There Has To Be) Something More Than Everything

Oh, everywhere. All around. Trees are harlequins, words are harlequins. So are situations and sums. Put two things together — jokes, images — and you get a triple harlequin. Come on! Play! Invent the world! Invent reality!

VLADIMIR NABOKOV

But there are things that have been torn away.
From all of us. And we need to collect the shadows,
the pain as it ghosts along the soul in faded fragments.
We need to put as many old pieces as we can together
to make something else entirely.
As many times as we have to and as long as it takes.

There is for instance this mourning
I've been running from for six years.
My blithe floating off to Mexico

sure that time was in abundant supply
and leaving Albie showing the nurses
how to find the veins in his arms.
Showing them access to the bloodstream
the way only a junkie could know it.
Leaving him with a splendid view
of the Texas hill country and his own
short-lived certainty of harlequins and
most of his heart that would soon fall apart
trussed up into a series of blips
staggering across a hospital monitoring screen.
Leaving him knowing which words are the last
and how they should be spoken.

The story of death is infinite in its variety
but the end is always the same.
This time it comes with the impersonal
scratching of a long distance line,
someone saying, *Sit down and listen. Albie's gone.*

I clutch the edge of a hard bed in a hot hotel room
in an ancient country where there is nothing
at this moment except a senseless dead-end present.
No past.   No future.   Downstairs in the courtyard
a woman with a face older than the first sun forgets
and shapes corn into cakes intended only for the living.
The jaguar leaves his temple stone and his godhood
    behind
and lets his claws and teeth go soft with mortality.
The orchid suspends its sweetness
high in the canopy of the jungle
as if there will be no tomorrow
as if yesterday the young bride had not

fixed love into her hair.
To have come this far to see time snag and eddy
around my closest cousin's still-warm body.
To have come this far to watch him finally
drain away in that slow-motion torrent
he had always claimed as his own rhythm.

Today is six years to the day he was buried.
I know because Albert just called to tell me
that he's a little bit drunk and
that he's cooked up a batch of chicken creole
and why don't I come on over
and the damn calendar never just folds its hands
and waits like the rest of us
and yesterday was Father's Day
this year an even uglier black mark
precisely setting apart the hours
between the Sunday his firstborn died
and the funeral on Monday.
And we talked about growing old
and how the body begins to falter
and about the new camper
that sleeps two comfortably
and when not in use can fold down
to only six inches on top of the car.

And about taking Lupe and Sister Julia
to their hometown in The Valley
to visit an old aunt.
And about how electrical engineers have impatiently
taken over the functions of real watchmakers
without having an inkling of how to order

the true passage of time.
And about the sons who are left.

And suddenly there it is.
Something more than everything.
Everywhere.   All around.
In the mundane inventions of our living
and laughing and grieving.
In the way we are somehow bound together
by this thing called family
that each of us celebrates so differently
but sometimes not so differently after all.
Just one stop on the way
to pick up a loaf of French bread
to go with the chicken.

E V A N G E L I N A   V I G I L - P I Ñ O N

Night Vigil

in the twilight hour all is still
all lights out
except for my nocturnal eyes, fluorescent
shining on *oscuridades*
spotlight rolling
exposing crevices on walls
shaded pastel surfaces
elongated door structures
furnishings converted into *bultos* by the darkness
como los que te espantaron cuando niña
"cúrala de susto"
dijo tu abuelita:
in your juvenile memory
four little broomstraws forming crosses
an egg, water

in night surroundings while others sleep
my heart thumps, off beat
absolutely refusing to align itself with time

ticking rhythmically
from faithful clock
marking time
advancing time
in night surroundings while others dream
I can taste my solitude

my imagination spins
images take form
I recall the splendor of beaches in the Caribbean
warmed by the sun
caressed by waters blue
I recall the powerful thrusts of the Atlantic
the Pacific
I envision beaches being swallowed up by night tide
the color of obsidian
moon illuminating rapture

I picture in my mind
receding waters
por la mañana
exposing sprinklings of starfish, urchins, seashell pedals
    pink
nocturnal creatures slithering, crawling, stretching
traces of last night's liquid passion
(what the stars will not tell)
realization anchored in this knowledge:

    the universe is immeasurable;
    the constellations shine so

thoughtglow spins into silvermist, then silverblack
then into live darkness

feelings, sensations have collected themselves back in-
    ward
to self-consuming origins
in depths of memories reconcealed

    images have disappeared before my very eyes
    like they were the tails of comets
    or paths of falling stars

        images have vanished in colorful flashes
        dash by dash
        like silk scarf streamers would ,
        into elegant skillful, white-gloved hands
        of a magician

consciousness retreats into my breathing body
I am back in this room
I feel calm awareness of heart pumping lifeblood rhyth-
    mically
my own body warmth sends chill through my bones
warmth regenerates
I breathe in stillness
with ease

solitude, darkness, quiet
envelop me once more
feelings of loneliness, forlornness gather in my chest

they weigh my heart
sentimiento slowly transforms into a focused thought—
spotlight rolling again
mind fluorescent, sensors beaming
surveillant

sideglance:
the sky glows opaque
window frames silhouette of tree with winter limbs
the branches are brittle, made so by the frost
they are silver-lined with moonmist
they are beautiful, elegant
they express artistry, magic

closing my eyes, I turn inward
I feel fluid, serene, peaceful
my mind lies potent with imagination
all is silent around me
I am by myself
I am singular
the night's presence cushions me
its embrace is pillow soft

como un indio
who in stillness detects stampede
of approaching herd
I detect
far off in the distance
an approaching train
its heavy rhythmic speed transmits velocity through my
     bones
its iron clanking sounds are muffled, sifted
by the night air thick with mist and fog
I hear its familiar whistle
its distant call slowly permeates through nightspace
it rings solitude
immense sadness engulfs me
it is upon me
but it quickly begins to fade

like a tumbleweed of sound
rolling by:
I wonder who this nighttrain traveler is
I wonder how he feels about this vast sea
of nocturnal singular existence

I pull multicolored quilt over my head
mind rests assured:
in the morning the sea will flow aquablue
sparkling and vibrant, activated by the sun
brilliance, inspiration
will explode from within the spirit, uncontained
but tonight
nocturnal naked eyes keep watch
beholding with awe
heart's inner vision:

moment's pause
del corazón
anchored in perennial motion
like cascades of the ocean waves
gushing
crowned with white lace liquid patterns
jeweled with watermist of pearls exquisite
crescents volatile, explosive
energía sculpted
by force of rolling tide

ENEDINA CÁSAREZ VÁSQUEZ

The
House
of
Quilts

IDIDN'T KNOW where I was and I didn't know that it was 1956, as dates and years were not important to me. It was late in the afternoon, and I was very weary from the three days of travel. Mom had again pulled us out of school and had told Ms. Manahan, our school principal that we were all going away to work and would not be coming back until the new school year. I was anxious to see the place where we were going to live. At least, I thought, we were going to stay, because it would be a shame to travel for three days looking for a place and then not stay. My mother and my brother and sister were in a big truck along with other families, all strangers, yet all going to the same place. We slept on quilts and that surprised me because I always thought that my grandmother was the only person who made quilts. There were quilts everywhere, and at night they looked like brightly colored fields with rolling hills and stacks of hair piled up in one straight line, the brightly colored threads weaving and changing colors, dividing up the land. Each quilt had its own quality, perhaps because each carried that family's history in every patch of cloth, just like mine carried my family's story.

The rain started when we passed something called "Chicago," but now the sun was out and it was very hot and dry. I loved the rain and I had enjoyed hearing the raindrops pound the canvas cover on the truck. Somehow time passes more quickly when one can make a tune with raindrops and the sounds of cars passing by. And that is how I passed the time, playing my own music to my very own self.

The truck had come to a stop at the end of a winding dirt road and the adults began to climb out—the men that is. I could hear voices and I tried not to listen because those were the instructions—when adults are talking, you do not listen. The men sounded as if they were walking away from the truck and I stood up to see what was going on.

Beyond the men I saw a beautiful, huge house, as white as the pages on my drawing tablet, with many windows and doors. I had never seen such a place in all of my life. The yard was endless and had so many trees I imagined that this was what a forest would look like. The air was filled with sunlight and the fresh smell of honeysuckle. As I stood there gazing at the house, I noticed Doña Isabelita was getting off the truck.

Doña Isabelita was a very fat woman—the largest person I had ever seen. She could hardly move, yet she always insisted on getting off the truck and we would all have to wait for her to climb back up, which was very funny to see. Like a pig trying to climb a fence. I often wished that she were more like my mother, who always obeyed and was very quiet and very thin. We were not allowed to laugh at Doña Isabelita, so all the children would cup their hands over their mouths and turn red in the face.

I watched as she approached the men who were now deep in conversation. She joined them and then let out a very loud scream. She was like a bowling ball about to make a strike. She began to wave her arms, and when she grabbed her husband, Don Lucio, by the throat, I knew that something worth watching was about to happen. His bones rattled under her firm grip. When the dust cleared, the men and Doña Isabelita walked back to the truck. It was time to unload. We were going to stay.

I

The place was Oconto, Wisconsin, and the house belonged to the farmer whose beets, greenbeans, and tomatoes we had been hired to pick. We were six families in the truck, and we were moving into the huge house surrounded by a sea of green. Six families as different as the patches that my grandmother used to make her quilts. But we became a quilt of people held together by the thread of our labor.

I was excited because everything was new, and I liked new places. Leaving the adults in deep conversation and planning, and my sisters playing near the truck, I began to look at everything. I noticed a big tree by the front of the house with branches that touched the sky, tall and important. As I stood gazing at it, my eyes caught something very strange. A pair of boots. They were just hanging there from one of the branches.

I thought to myself, "What are those boots doing up there and how did they get there?" The afternoon sun was warm and the people around me were too busy to notice them. I had to know where they had come from, but no one knew or cared. "Could they have belonged to someone who had lived in the house?" I asked myself. "Is his ghost in the house?" I wondered if the owner of the boots had been lynched, like the men in the stories my mother had told me about the Klan and how they terrorized her brothers when she was little and growing up in Selma, Texas. His hanging could be possible I thought. After all, I had seen a hanging on television so I knew that it was possible. These things could happen. Already there were ghosts haunting me.

I found it hard to concentrate on anything else but those boots. They just hung there without an explanation: People should not put boots on a tree like that without explaining where they came from, because whoever finds the boots will not know how they got there, and they will worry about them for the rest of their life.

Standing there trying to solve the puzzle of the boots, I became aware of the argument between Doña Isabelita and Don Lucio. They were shouting at each other again, and I decided that I should go and see why she was threatening to kill him.

The men had divided up the house and there had been room for only five families. Don Lucio, being kind hearted, had volunteered to move his family into the chicken coop. Now, I knew why she was trying to kill him, but I didn't understand why she was so upset, because to me it seemed that the chicken coop was a nice place, a little dirty but nice. It had two doors and one very long window that had chicken wire instead of glass. Doña Isabelita kept yelling at her husband, screaming that she would never forgive him as long as she lived. "I wish I had never married you and had all those twelve kids. . . . If Mother were here, she and I would give you a good beating. You are no good, Lucio! You are worthless!" She went into the coop and began to throw things out the door. She was a strong fat woman with a broom in her hand. "I would rather die than live in a place like this," she screamed. "It is not fit for chickens, much less for my children. You are no good Lucio. You are just no good."

I I

Together Don Lucio and Doña Isabelita looked like the number ten. He was tall and very skinny while she was fat and very round. They had twelve children and in the fields they looked like chickens scratching the dirt. Don Lucio had learned to ignore his wife, and she had learned that she was the one on whose shoulders rested the responsibility of rearing the children. He was Jack Sprat and she was the tub of lard. But Don Lucio was special to me. He was a poet and could write poems in his head and say them out loud; he wrote poems about everything, and I loved to listen to him make up poems about each one of us living in the big house. He made a poem about me, and

I loved the sound of my name in a poem. He was gentle and soft spoken, and his wife's constant nagging never seemed to bother him; I think it actually helped him write better poetry. The one thing that I did not like about him was that he would cough all the time and spit out blood.

Doña Isabelita vowed that she would never forgive Don Lucio for having moved his family into the chicken coop. Every time they argued, which was everyday, she would rant and rave that as long as she lived she would never forget what he had done, and then she would proceed to call him names and hit him with the broom. Nothing ever bothered Don Lucio.

I I I

The family that owned the truck that brought us to Ocanto had the best rooms in the house, and their door was used only by them. Their last name was Abelardo, and they had one old daughter, about thirty-five, a teenage son, and a very fat little girl about my age. This family was very strange. They were very white and looked Anglo, but they were Mexican. The man had blue eyes and so did his wife. The oldest daughter was not married, and this concerned all of the women. She was the topic of most of the gossip. Mr. Abelardo's son had only one eye, and this scared me very much; every time I asked about it, no one would ever tell me what happened to his eye. His eye lid barely closed over the hole, and my mother kept us in line by telling us that if we didn't behave we would wind up just like that poor boy. One day some of the boys chased him, and they threw him to the ground; they opened his eyelids, and we all saw a white ball, staring at us. That's all that was in the socket, one white ball.

I didn't like the little girl. Her name was Irene, and I didn't play with her very much. She was too pink, and I tried to avoid her. Fat lips, she had fat pink lips, red cheeks, and blue eyes. She looked funny.

The Abelardos, the white-colored family, worked in the fields with us, but their section had no hills on it, and they stayed close to the truck. This way, they could see if anyone was sneaking off to get water or to rest. When the flat summer sun burned our backs, we could see the family resting under the truck and having lunch, while we had our lunch in the stark naked green ocean. They reported every infraction to the owner of the farm; they told us when to eat and when we could go behind a tree to go to the bathroom. Mr. Abelardo's wife did not go out into the fields. Her place was at home, and she stayed inside the house all day. She never spoke to us, especially not to the women, and she never joined in the gossip or the parties.

I V

One family had just one child: Teodoro and his wife and their retarded son. The wife was lazy, at least everyone said she was. I would hear the women talk about her, and they all agreed that she was lazy and up to no good. Teodoro liked to drink every day, and he liked to chase after Don Abelardo's daughter, Refugia. Doña Isabelita kept us all informed about the goings on between Refugia and Teodoro because they met late at night behind the chicken coop. At lunch time in the fields the women would get together and ask Doña Isabelita to tell them what had gone on the night before and what she had heard or seen. Doña Isabelita was very popular with the women. I listened too, and I wondered where she hid so that Teodoro and Refugia would not see her. After all, she was such a fat woman that it would be hard not to see her.

Teodoro's wife did not do much of anything. She always dressed as though she were going somewhere—red rouge, red lipstick and red long fingernails. A clown, she looked like a clown. In the fields she would wear colorful dresses, and I thought that it was quite dumb because it was hard enough work to pick tomatoes when one is wearing pants. She always sneered at the other women; she knew that they were all talking about her. She would spend her time sitting by the window looking out. Her son was very mischievous, and he would pester everyone. She would watch him from the window and if he was doing something wrong, she would holler at the top of her voice, "Teodoro! Mira Junior, Teodoro!" She would not come down and take care of her son; it was her husband's job to do that. They always argued, and sometimes the whole house would hear them and no one would get much sleep then.

They left Oconto before the picking season was over because she found out about Teodoro and Refugia. They had a big fight and they left. I was glad that they left because I was getting tired of hearing them argue all the time. After they were gone my sister and I would take turns standing in the window of the empty room yelling, "Teodoro, Mira Junior, Teodoro!"

V

The Jimenez family was also very strange. Mr. Jimenez was very young and his wife was very old, and they had one child. They were not married, and my father was very bothered by that fact. My mother and the other women were also curious about the strange couple. Mr. Jimenez looked like he was the woman's son; my mother said he looked half her age. This was all very interesting to the rest of the women and generated much talk among them. When we would board the truck to go out into the fields, I could see everyone's eyes looking at the couple; it always gave me a funny feeling because no one ever said anything to them. Everyone just looked, and the women gossiped later.

Their son was all right, there was nothing wrong with him, but his father was very cruel to him. He would beat him for no reason and then tie him to the tree out in the yard and make him stay there all day—then go out and beat him again and take him inside the house. We never said anything because it was their business. Once we didn't see the son all day, and we later found out that his father had tied him to the bed post and had refused to feed him that whole day; he was very obedient, and his mother never defended him or touched him. The father would blame him for everything, but we never saw the boy be rude to him or get into trouble. The boy never complained to his father or to any one of us, and he was fun when he wasn't tied up. The boy, whose name was Tony, was ten years old and he had the habit of winking his eye, sort of like someone who has a twitch. This made me very nervous because when I saw him do that my eye twitched, too. My father nicknamed him *"Puntería,"* which means sharp eye. We liked playing with him, but we also always felt sorry for all those beatings he took. Sometimes when he was tied to the tree, he looked like a little, thirsty puppy.

His mother didn't know how to paint her face; she just put on all the makeup and probably didn't even know she looked like an old, tired clown. She had red tomatoes for cheeks and red strawberries for lips. The lines of her eyebrows were drawn with a black pencil, and she looked horrible. I never understood why she wore so much paint on her face. The woman and her husband argued all the time; the arguments always scared Puntería because he knew that it would only be settled when he got his beating. He would hide in our stall until it was all over or until his father came and dragged him away, rope in hand.

V I

Then there was the Ramirez family, Pedro and his wife Josefa. It seemed to me that he was a very wise man because all of the men sought his advice, especially when there were problems about working conditions. He was the one who would approach Don Abelardo and get things resolved. They never spoke much otherwise. Pedro would mostly nod and speak little gentle words. One of the things that bothered me about Don Pedro was that one of his hands was missing, and I always had a problem because everytime I saw him I tried not to look at his hand, which of course meant that I spent a lot of time looking at it. The other children made fun of his missing hand when he was not around. My father and the other men called him *"El Morrito,"* which meant that he only had a stump for a hand. He and his wife did not mix with the other families very much. They were hard workers and they kept to themselves.

When the men divided up the rooms of the house, my father selected the horse stall for us to live in. My mother was very upset, but she did not complain, unlike the loud Doña Isabelita, because she knew that she should not. It was her job to do the best that she could with what she had. My mother always found ways to make do, and she made us feel at home in that stall. She could make something out of nothing.

My brother, Tomás, was a teenager, and he liked to dress in jeans and a black leather jacket, which my father hated. Tomás used lots of grease in his hair, and my father was always after him to cut it and not look like a hoodlum. Tomás was always getting into trouble because he liked the farmer's daughter. My mother told him that he shouldn't even think of dating the girl, and her warning made him very angry. My mother always said it was not his place to date a white girl, that it would get us all into trouble. But Tomás did not care, and sometimes I would see him and the girl kissing under a tree that was in the back yard.

My little sister Josie and I were content to play with the other children and to wait for the bus to take us to school. She and I wanted to be like Annette Funicello, and we actually thought we looked like her. Sometimes after school we were allowed to watch "The Mickey Mouse Show" on the Abelardo's television, and it was like Christmas for us. We were dreamers, Josie and me, and we wanted to grow up to be famous and never be poor again. We held on to that dream. Josie would always get into fights with the other kids, and she would tell them that when she was rich and famous she would not talk to them because she would be too busy signing autographs for all her fans.

My older sister Irene was best friends with one of Doña Isabelita's daughters, and they used to dress in button-up sweaters and skirts that had poodles on them. They were always dancing together and trying to imitate the girls on "American Bandstand." The two of them spent hours fixing their bobby socks just right and playing records on the record player.

I liked living in the stall. It was spacious and nice, or at least I thought so. To me it was a beautiful living space, but my mother cried most of the time while she was cleaning it; and I never understood why. We used wooden crates as chairs, and my father made a wooden table for our kitchen area. Mother took rope and stretched it across the opening of each of the stalls and hung our quilts to make it look like we each had our own room. To me it was a beautiful scene. Quilts were our walls, and we knew every inch of them. It was like my grandmother was there with us, her hands at work decorating our lives in that place in Oconto.

VIII

The barn where we lived was very pretty, but the man for whom we worked had an even prettier house. His house was made of red brick and had white windows and doors.

His was a dairy farm, and he owned many cows. I enjoyed watching him milk the cows, and sometimes he would let me feed them. I wanted to spend the rest of my life on that farm and be rich and famous.

Sometimes my mother would send me to buy eggs from the farmer. The walk was a long one but I enjoyed it because I would daydream and imagine myself to be many different things. I liked the sun and the flowers along the road and the peacefulness of the place, but I was always embarrassed when cars passed by because the people of that area knew we were migrant workers and the children would always yell cruel things at me. It was funny because they would yell in English, thinking that I could not understand them, but I knew what they were calling me. I would look down at the road at those times, knowing that one day I would grow up and be *somebody* and then they would no longer call me names or laugh at me.

The farmer owned the cooperative grocery store where we bought our food on credit. The store was big and had everything from clothes to canned goods. We and the other families went there to buy food and clothing, and the farmer would charge the items on our "family account."

When the picking season was over and it was time for us to leave, all the families went to the store to collect our pay and to pay off our accounts. I remember that day very well because everyone became angry. My father was upset because after the farmer subtracted our store bill from our pay, the farmer gave him only seventy-two dollars. My father could not believe that we had spent so much on so little and that all the work that we had done was paid with seventy-two dollars. We barely had enough to meet our expenses on the ride back home. All the other families had the same problem, but the ones who really had a problem were the Lucios. As it turned out, they owed the farmer money. So we all tried to give him some of our money to help them pay so that the farmer would not call the police. But Don Lucio, being a proud man, refused the money and the help, and he and his family remained behind on the farm to work off the debt. My sister Irene cried because her friend had to stay behind.

The Abelardos, the white-colored Mexican family that owned the truck, were very lucky. They made enough money to pay the farmer and had enough left over to buy their son a car.

The farmer had two children, a boy and a girl. They had swings and bicycles and roller skates. How I wished that I could have played with their roller skates. I didn't much care for the swings, but I would have liked to play with their skates. But the girl was older, and she played with my brother Tomás, and the boy was too busy riding his bike. The girl liked to wear poodle skirts like my sister Irene.

They had a beautiful garden with strawberry plants and apple trees. I just loved strawberries; it was fun to learn how they grew and when to pick them. I would look at the strawberries from across the fence. They were so red and juicy that they made my mouth water. But all I could do was look. The apple trees were tall and laden with apples, some green, some red. One day the farmer saw me and the other children sitting on the fence looking at the apples, pretending to count them, and he asked us if we wanted some. We jumped at the chance to get some of the apples and sang out a loud Yes! He told us that we could pick up only the ones that were on the ground and not to touch the ones on the trees. Even though some were rotten and some were bruised, we gathered them all and took them home in a basket. Mother cut out all the bad parts and made some delicious apple pies. My mother could always make something out of nothing in that house of quilts.

Uncle Teo's Shorthand Cookbook

Everyone knows that Cubans speak in shorthand. Part of each word is pronounced, but the rest must be imagined. So when Cubans go into exile, our overseas friends often seize us by the shoulders and shake us, saying "Calm yourself, slow down. No one can understand you."

We calm ourselves, briefly. Then, gradually, fresh momentum is gathered, the voice accelerates, becomes a race car, a runaway train, a barrel rushing over a waterfall, speeding and plummeting toward the inevitable crash. Then silence: pensive, mournful, nostalgic. Wistful silence. Friends beg us to speak, to tell our stories, to repeat the chants of betrayal. And we do.

Take Uncle Teo. He's not really our uncle, just another neighbor, but we call him Uncle to distinguish him

from Teófilo down the street, and Teodoro who moved to
Spain, and Teofrasto in Costa Rica, and all of our cousins
who still live in Cuba: Teobaldo, Teócrito, Teodosio . . .

Uncle Teo talks faster than any other Cuban on earth,
especially when he's giving you a recipe. Maybe it's because he knows that no one can cook his recipes anyway.
We used to see him on TV in Havana, and now, imagine
it yourself, here we are in Florida, neighbors and equals,
even though he was once the most famous chef in Cuba,
and we are just ordinary housewives who can barely whip
up the kind of thing one would refer to as "party food."

Uncle Teo lives alone now. You can tell he's lonely.
We all are, all the families split up by the revolution,
everyone fleeing this way or that, falling like windblown
leaves and settling in different countries.

Uncle Teo is retired now. He stays home all day,
cooking and drinking. Everyone knows he doesn't eat
much, so we go over there to watch him cook; then of
course he invites us to taste a little, and naturally we do.
His kind of retirement is different than the American's.
In English, you know, retired sounds like someone is
lying down all the time, sleeping or at least dozing off
from time to time. But in Spanish! *Jubilarse,* you see? Jubilated. A chance to get down to the real business of celebrating. In Spanish, when you are old you are wise, so
that is certainly something to celebrate, isn't it?

When it comes to cooking, Uncle Teo is as wise as
they get. He can make a stew out of nothing but beans,
and people will come from miles around to tell him his
house smells like heaven.

He kept his cookbook program going for a long time
after the revolution, considering that there was hardly any
food left to cook and certainly no need for fancy recipes.

Back in the '50s "Teo's Cookbook" was the best television cooking show on earth. He would alternate traditional Cuban dishes with modern delicacies, molded aspics, and gourmet pastas. Uncle Teo attracted recipes the way magnets attract iron filings. First he would taste something in a fancy restaurant far away, France or Italy, and then they would show him coming back and next thing you knew, there it was all arranged and displayed on television, with the ingredients passing you by so fast that you never knew what had hit you, a cyclone or Uncle Teo.

Back then the program was just called "Teo's Cookbook." Later the revolutionary government changed it to "Teo's Shorthand Cookbook," to show how a clever cook could make do with less.

In the old days Uncle Teo would start out right, with lists of spices a mile long. Every main dish began the same way: olive oil from Spain, onions, bell peppers, garlic, tomatoes, pimientos, cumin, oregano, dry sherry, and one leaf from the laurel bay tree. From there you could branch out, adding salted codfish, cubed pork, or saffron rice with chicken. To make fried cow you left out the tomato and added lime juice. For stuffed pot roast you needed potatoes, ham, green olives, and the juice of a sour orange from Sevilla.

Seafood dishes were always the most complicated. Islanders find this natural, because we know how many kinds of fish live in the sea. *Zarzuela,* for instance, requires twenty-two ingredients. Don't ask me why it gets its name from the comic opera; maybe it's because the rest of us look funny when we try to cook something that complex, but Uncle Teo always made it look so elegant and graceful that we felt inspired to give the mess a try.

Swordfish is pretty simple to prepare, but the procedure for red snapper stuffed with bread and lobster just goes on and on. Since the program only lasted half an hour, Uncle Teo had to whip up those dishes ahead of time, then show them off to the camera and rattle away at the list of ingredients, hoping to finish on time for the Campbell's soup commercial.

The revolution ended all that. Hardly any ingredients were available, there were no commercials or canned soup, or even spices, unless you grew them yourself. You had to get Sevilla oranges out of your own back yard, and there wasn't any Spanish olive oil; you were lucky if you could find a little lard or chicken fat.

Which reminds me of *frituras,* the most Cuban of foods, and certainly my personal favorites. Uncle Teo always was a *fritura* specialist. He showed us that all we have to do is smash something, or grind it or puree it, then drop it by spoonfuls into deep, sizzling oil until golden brown on all sides, remove it with a slotted spoon, drain on absorbent paper, and serve hot with salt and lime juice. Uncle Teo used to do this with crabmeat or black-eyed peas, or ham, or garbanzos. He called the ham "croquettes" instead of fritters, and he made the garbanzos fancy by serving them with avocado sauce instead of lime juice. One family can go through an awful lot of fritters in an afternoon, so he always advised us to make twice as much as we thought we needed and plan on plenty of unexpected company both between meals and when we sat down to dinner. He said there was nothing wrong with spending two or three hours eating dinner if you had good company, but of course that was before the revolution when all the cousins still lived close enough to show up uninvited.

The best thing about those days (Uncle Teo now calls

them the old Cuba, but the rest of us think of them as the real Cuba) was you didn't have to eat your vegetables. Salad never meant lettuce. Salad was sliced avocados with fresh fruit or cold fish or cold ham or cold chicken. Uncle Teo had a lot of fun showing salads on TV, because he knew no one would eat them if they came from France and had lots of greens. He liked to tease.

Then came the era of eggs. After the revolution all we had was rice and beans and eggs. So Uncle Teo would feature baked eggs with potatoes, fried eggs with rice, scrambled eggs plain, and omelettes with beans. You could see that he was really bored with those shorthand programs. He would stand up there in front of the camera and reminisce about eggs baked in dry sherry with deveined shrimp or chopped ham and asparagus tips and baby sweet peas.

Desserts were a problem too, especially when everyone ran out of milk. This was after most of the dairy farmers were sent to forced labor camps so their farms could be collectivized. Then, to make it worse, that whimsical revolution went and loaded the whole island with big strong prize bulls, while slaughtering all the cows for meat! By the time the bureaucrats realized what they had done, it was too late. Uncle Teo couldn't keep telling people about fried milk squares (my favorite), coconut *flan,* or old-fashioned *natilla* custard with its crust of sugar and cinnamon made by heating a clothes iron over coals and then pressing it down to burn the sugar.

He started working with whatever fruit was in season. There were oranges dunked in rum and garnished with wild mint leaves. Coconut crisps baked with cinnamon sticks. Sugared mango. Sugared guava. And of course there were fritters: banana fritters, sweet potato fritters, coconut fritters.

Pastries fell by the wayside. So did cakes and home-made ice creams and fruit served with cheese.

Actually, nothing really bad ever happened to Uncle Teo in Cuba (unlike the rest of us). His program was still popular, more than ever in fact. Because we had so little to cook with, we needed his help imagining how to get by. He was never arrested or accused of disloyalty or sent to the labor camps or humiliated in public or beaten by the secret police. He simply ran out of ingredients and grew discouraged. In English, that is what you would call it: dis-couraged. In Spanish we say *disanimated*—listless, lethargic. His speech slowed and his cooking skills simmered. I believe the problem was he was lonely, because so many of his friends and family members were leaving, one by one or being arrested or were afraid to visit because you never knew who you could talk to without being mis-understood or reported. The worst thing about the revo-lution, much worse than the shortages and hardships, was the way you couldn't trust anybody anymore, not even your own relatives. You had to always be on guard, always separate. There was no more family or community or neighborliness. Everything was revolution this and revo-lution that. There was a lot of rhetoric about equality and justice, but of course it wasn't true, none of it. How could it be? Not when farmers were being sent away so that uni-versity students from the city could be trained to farm, and not when prize bulls were being imported while cows were being massacred so milk production could be in-creased. Those kinds of plans never work out. Sooner or later everyone realizes that the people in charge don't have the foggiest idea what they're doing. You can invent a recipe from scratch, but not a government. It has to have some basis in fact, some outline for justice.

Now, in exile, talking a thousand miles per hour, Uncle Teo can once again show you how to make a real Cuban goat stew or a spit-roasted pig or corn fritters, garlic soup, octopus salad, stuffed meat loaf, banana omelettes, rum-baked shrimp, fried bread, fish pudding, lamb and bacon stew . . .

Of course, Uncle Teo won't cook on TV anymore, not in Spanish or English, even though he could. He's had offers from local cable and Univisión. He just likes to cook by himself now, without a camera, and people go to his house to watch. Hardly anyone ever tries to copy any of his recipes exactly, not unless they know shorthand, but they get the general drift; and usually they go home and try to do something similar without a written recipe. At Uncle Teo's house, just watching him is enough to become an inspired cook. I always come home and whip up my own masterpieces. I try setting a recipe to music or doing it in rhyme, or I arrange the food on ceramic plates decorated with hibiscus flowers, and I take a photograph before sitting down to eat.

Uncle Teo drinks a lot now, some say too much. Big pitchers of orange daiquiris, pineapple gin, grenadine with apricot brandy. He mixes rum with beer, and curaçao with vermouth, and he makes the best banana and rum milkshakes you can imagine, and the best guava nectar champagne, pineapple juice vodka, and orange maraschino liqueur. Always with freshly squeezed lime juice from real tropical limes, the kind you can only find in Cuba or south Florida or in the memory of an old man who was always the best at everything he did.

The rest of us love to drink at Uncle Teo's house and watch the food take form and listen to the shower of words as they splash all around at hurricane speed.

No one ever tells Uncle Teo to slow down anymore. He knows where he's going, and he seems to be in a hurry to get there, so why should we interfere with his pleasure along the way?

Watching Uncle Teo cook and listening to him talk, out of necessity you learn a little shorthand. When you go home and find you only have five of the fifteen ingredients, you make do with spiced-up leftovers, but your memory holds his wonderful table in photographic detail: the napkins folded into flower shapes, the roast pig holding an orange in its mouth, the seafood salads arranged on an ornamental island of banana leaves trimmed into little palm tree shapes.

You pretend there are plenty of relatives invited to the meal, hundreds, and friends too, neighbors, even strangers. No shortages, nothing rationed or absent, not even love, especially not love. That's what Uncle Teo says, make do with less, but pretend it's all there: bountiful, generous, not the way it turned out, but the way it should be, the way God planned it—big families sitting down together in a garden, each person tasting little bits of a thousand different fruits, but always saving that special one for later.

GLORIA ANZALDÚA

Holy Relics

for Judy Grahn and V. Sackville-West

We are the holy relics,
the scattered bones of a saint,
the best loved bones of Spain.
We seek each other.

City of Ávila,
88 crenellated towers crowning a low hill.
A silent landscape rises toward indigo mountains,
empty save for clumps of broom and tormented ilex.
Here and there strange stones
like prehistoric ruins.
A granite city in a dour land,
with a cathedral for a fortress.
A land where no mists soften the rocks,
where light is relentless.

When she* died, flesh of our bones,
they buried her at the Alba de Tormes

*Teresa de Cepeda Dávila y Ahumada

50 miles west of Ávila.
They finally buried her
in her patched and shabby habit.
Buried her in her threadworn veil.
Bricked her in a wall of grey stone.

Nine months she lay in the grey stone.
Nine months she lay quietly.
Her daughters, the nuns of Alba, came to her daily—

came to that bricked-up place in the wall.
From that place issued a scent
to which they could give no name.
From within that tomb
issued a sound to which they could give no name.

Day by day they waited.
They waited for the good father Gracian,
Teresa's beloved confessor,
waited to tell him of that scent and of that sound.

Entombed nine months.
Four days it took them.
Four days in silence, in secret.
The nuns held the torches
while Father and friar shoveled.
The nuns held the torches
then cleared away the rubble.
At last the hallowed moment,
the coffin pulled from the cavern.
The moment when the lid is broken,
when the coffin is opened.
They gazed at last at their beloved:

spider webs netted black hair to eyebrows,
earth clotted her arched nostrils.
They gazed and gazed at their beloved.
The nuns of Alba removed her mouldy habit,
with knives scraped away the earth clinging to her skin,
looked their fill,
then wrapped her in clean linen.
The good Father drew near,
lifted her left hand as if to kiss it,
placed a knife under her wrist
and from her rigid arm he severed it.
The father Teresa had loved stood smiling,
hugging her hand to his body.

> We are the holy relics,
> the scattered bones of a saint,
> the best loved bones of Spain.
> We seek each other.

Two years she lay in her tomb.
Pero para los santos no hay descanso,
for saints there is no rest.
Another priest fell upon her tomb
to claim her holy body for Ávila.
At midnight he sent the nuns
to the upper choir to sing matins.
Then quietly removed the bricked-up stones,
quietly reopened the tomb.
The mysterious scent and her unspoiled face
(a little more dried than before) greeted him.
And bright red as if freshly soaked
was the cloak of white bunting

that had staunched the flow from her mouth at her
    deathbed.

It stained whatever piece of cloth touched it.
The scent drifted to the upper choir
drawing the nuns down to the tomb like flies to honey
in time to see Father Gregorio de Naciancene
insert his knife under the truncated arm,
in time to see the blade pass through flesh
as if through cheese.
And flinging the arm at the nuns of Alba
as one would a bone to a dog
he detained them long enough
to mount the shroud on horseback
and gallop away.

          We are the holy relics,
          the scattered bones of a saint,
          the best loved bones of Spain.
          We seek each other.

Through the bitter winds of Ávila
Teresa raced from the grave.
She traveled at night,
and briefly during the run she stopped
to resuscitate a dying child
with the edge of her bloodstained rag,
paused to heal the fiery eyes of a shepherd.
Toward the 88 towers and their indented embrasures
they galloped.
Through streets of Ávila,
past high-walled houses where black eyes behind lattices

stared down at the shroud riding on horseback.
Into San José convent he took her
and placed her upon a bright carpet.
A small group gathered around,
each held a flaming torch.
All were crying.

Later, one witness described the corpse:
"The body is erect, though bent a little forward,
as with old people.
It can be made to stand upright,
if propped with a hand between the shoulders,
and this is the position they hold it
when it is to be dressed or undressed,
as though it were alive.
The colour of the body
is of the colour of dates; the face darker,
because the veil became stuck to it,
and it was maltreated more than the rest;
nevertheless, it is intact.
And even the nose is undamaged.
The head has retained all its hair.
The eyes, having lost their vital moisture,
are dried up, but the eyelids are perfectly preserved.
The moles on her face retain their little hairs.
The mouth is tightly shut and cannot be opened.
The shoulder from which the arm was severed
exudes a moisture that clings to the touch
and exhales the same scent as the body."

News of her disinterment spread.
It reached the ears of the Duke of Alba.

He petitioned the pope for the immediate return of the
    body.

Once more Teresa traveled,
traveled at night
away from the 88 towers.
Through the bitter winds of Ávila
she galloped toward her grave.
Abbots on well-fed mules turned and gaped.
Peasants stopped thrashing their corn.
They followed the mysterious smell
and saw it cure a monk's malaria.
Through the gates of Alba
the priest rode.
He laid the shroud before the nuns.
Raising his torch high,
he uncovered the body.
"If these be the remains of your Foundress
acknowledge them before God."

Again she lay quietly
in her granite grave.
The third time she was exhumed,
a crowd gathered round,
eyes coveting her body.
Over-ardent fingers—
fingers that once had loved her—
pinched off pieces of her flesh.
A priest raised her one remaining hand,
gave a sharp twist snapping off two fingers.
Another grasped her right foot
and blessing her

severed it from her ankle.
A third fell upon her breast
and from her side
plucked three ribs.
Scraps of her bones they sold
to the aristocracy for money.
They auctioned tiny pieces of her fingernails
and one small white tooth.

Again they laid her in her grey stone grave.
And priests fell upon her body.
Her dried carnal husk
could still be torn into morsels.
They cut off her head,
laid it on a cushion of crimson satin
embroidered with silver and gold.
Like a crippled bird it lay,
left eye gouged out,
right eye protruding through full lashes,
its black lone gaze frozen.

A fifth time they dug her up years later.
A gaping hole where her heart had been ripped out
to be placed in a reliquary.
Three centuries later physicians would examine it,
would find a wound an inch and a half in length,
the edges of the wound charred
as though by a burning iron.
Above the high altar at Alba,
the fifth and final resting place,
lie the remains of a woman.

• *Gloria Anzaldúa* •

We are the holy relics,
the scattered bones of a saint,
the best loved bones of Spain.
We seek each other.

DEBORAH PAREDEZ

Tía María

TÍA MARÍA, everybody's saying she's addicted to
el Bingo, y quién sabe qué about the devil leading
her to the gambling. Amá prays for Tía María to git closer
to God and to find a man to set her straight. Me, I think
Tía María probly jus' likes the way all those Ping-Pong
balls with the numbers painted on them tumble around
and around and around in the little cage that Ernesto, he's
the Bingo Caller, turns and turns con sus big strong arms.
Also I think Tía María likes the way Ernesto yells
"Ohhhh 52" real loud in his deep voice all sexylike. Yeah
I jus' think Tía likes the way Ernesto yells. Ain't nothing
wrong with that, I think, pero today Tía is in the real hot
water porque it's Christmas and she was 'posed to be
bringing some more tamales and here it is already 7:00 at
night and she hasn't even called ni nada. We finally jus'
ate and opened all the presents with all my other tías and
cousins whispering and everything about how Tía María
din't even show up for Mass this morning and that she's
for sure going the devil's way now and this and that y

98

quién sabe qué. My cousin Lety, she's bigger than me and pura mentirosa, that's what I think, anyway, Lety is whispering to me, "Ay, that Tía María, she ain't up to no good, I tell you. Fíjate, Dolores," she's telling me, "I heard Tía Licha say that she heard from her friend at work que Tía María was at el Bingo every night the last two weeks, even on the night of El Día de La Virgen! Ay qué mujer! Can you believe it? I'm telling you, she ain't up to no good." Lety is talking y talking, her face all like a bunch of scribbles on a blackboard that I jus' wish I could erase. Me, I just nod and smile. Nod and smile. I don't say nothing back. Besides I'm too busy thinking about those Ping-Pong balls tumbling around in that little cage como palomitas flying around waiting to be free.

I know all about the Bingo 'cause Tía María has chosen me as her secret keeper. "Oyes, Dolores, don't tell tu amá que I went to el Bingo last night. OK?" Tía María always says to me, and then she gives me a dollar bill to hide in my shoe for when we go to the ice house and I can buy some of that sour candy that I love to eat and that makes Lety's face all like a prune with her mouth all squished up like a smushed bug on the windshield of Apá's truck. Tía María tells me all her Bingo secrets. I'm like the pocket in her old wool coat that she keeps in her cedar chest that smells real funny like old people or something. Anyway, that coat pocket is where she hides all the money she wins from the Bingo. Me, I'm like that pocket, all hidden, because I'm like a place where she hides all her secrets, like the story of that time she was needing the "B4" to get the picture frame, and I don't mean a real picture frame; that's a Bingo term, it's where you try to cover all the spaces on the edges of your card so it looks kinda like a picture frame. Anyway, she was jus' needing that

"B4" and she was going to win the three hundred dollar cash prize, and so she told me that she started praying "Dear Jesus please let me get the B4," and she was praying to St. Anthony, too (he's the one you pray to when you lose something), so I guess it made sense that Tía María was praying to St. Anthony because she was trying to win back all the money she had already lost. So she was praying and praying and saying "B4 B4, C'mon B4" and she said Ernesto looked over at her and gave her a wink like he knew she was praying for the "B4" 'cause the next thing he called out was "B4." "Can you believe it, Dolores? Ooojale, hombre!" she had said, all happy because Jesus and St. Anthony and Ernesto had helped her win the three hundred dollars. And she gives me another dollar to hide in my shoe for when we go to the store later. And I'm thinking with all these men helping her, Tía María don't really need no husband like Amá and everybody is always saying.

But now I am starting to get a little worried because already it's almost 8:00, and I'm thinking something bad (ojalá que no!) might have happened to Tía. Everybody else, they're jus' mad because they wanted more tamales. Luckily, Tía Licha brought a couple extra dozen. With Amá and everybody else working at their jobs so much, we mostly jus' buy our Christmas tamales these days. Nobody's got time to be making them from scratch, they say. Lara's Tortillería on the corner of Guadalupe Street and South Domingo is where everybody who knows anything about tamales goes to place their Christmas orders, but mostly we buy our tamales from Mrs. Treviño who still makes tamales at home. We buy them from her porque Amá says, "Pobrecita Señora Treviño, she ain't got no husband no more ever since he ran off con esa gringa named Darlene . . ." or something like that. "Y los hijos d'ella," Amá keeps on saying, "her kids don't help her or nothing. It's like the devil is with those damn kids." Mostly, Amá thinks the devil is with anybody she doesn't like or who plays Bingo. Amá's not the only one who thinks this, though. All of the other tías are always saying que Tía María is going with the devil to the Bingo because she ain't got no man, because she ain't got no family, 'cept Amá, her sister. "Pobrecita Lupita," that's Amá, "Pobrecita Lupita," they're always saying, all feeling sorry for Amá for having such a wild sister who goes to the Bingo con el diablo. And the whole time I'm thinking "pobrecita me" always having to feel sorry for everybody all the time and having to do too many chores. Pobrecita me, more like it.

And just when I'm feeling all sad and starting to put on the "mala cara" that Amá can't stand, Tía María comes in from the garage door, her heels going ssslaaap ssslaaap ssslaaap on the linoleum. She's whispering to me, "Oyes, Dolores, don't tell tu Amá, pero the Bingo Paradise on Jacksonville Road was having a special today, a Christmas Bingo they called it, and they were raffling off turkeys and everything. So I just had to go for a little while. Ernesto was there calling out the numbers with that deep voice of his, all man y todo. Fíjate Dolores, I won a butterball and fifty dollars. I got so excited I gave away all of Mrs. Treviño's tamales to my girlfriends at el Bingo!" And she is laughing and giving me a dollar bill to hide in my shoe. Then Amá and my other tías come in, and everybody gets all quiet and everything. The only one who's making any noise is Lety who's still whispering and whispering and Tía María, whose heels are going ssslaaap ssslaaap ssslaaap all the way across Amá's kitchen floor. With my cousin Lety still saying, "Ay, qué chihuahua, Tía María ain't up to no good, hombre. I'm telling you." And me just nodding and smiling. Nodding and smiling. "Yeah. No good, hombre," I'm thinking, "No. Good."

LUCHA CORPI

Four,
Free,
and
Illegal

I HAVE ALWAYS considered myself quite fortunate, for I spent the first eight years of my life in a
small community that fostered the creation, performance,
and appreciation of music and poetry, in addition to sto-
rytelling.

Located in the southern part of the state of Veracruz,
near the border with Tabasco, Jáltipan had a population
of about two thousand when I was born.

Although we enjoyed the use of electricity, we lacked
other modern conveniences. Since there was no tap water,
for example, people caught rainfall in large drums for
washing and bathing. Folks who could afford it paid
water carriers to bring cans of drinking water to their
doorsteps from the natural springs outside town.

Twice a week, Tirso, the water carrier, brought the

spring water to my grandmother's house. Sometimes Tirso would let my brother Víctor and me sit on his mules while he carried the cans inside.

Water carriers were famous for being among the toughest and most foul-tongued men in the region. Our Tirso was no exception. But unlike other water carriers, he delighted in teaching the children in town some of his favorite colorful expressions. Víctor and I were only five and three years old, respectively, but we were Tirso's star pupils.

Being a great deal more cautious than I, Víctor did not use this kind of colorful language in front of our parents, and he suggested that I follow his example, a warning that I, naturally, didn't heed. I filled up with those forbidden words, as if they were mangoes or guavas—meaty, sensual, sweet. Encouraged by my aunt's and cousins' chuckles, I practiced my newly acquired vocabulary quite often.

During one of those practice sessions, my mother heard me. "I'll wash your mouth with soap if I ever hear you use bad language again," my mother warned—then added, "I promise you."

I gave her innumerable opportunities to keep her "promise," and she did. That year, I was the three-year-old with the cleanest, though not necessarily the purest, tongue in town.

Had it not been for the discovery of a recently installed jukebox in the nearby bar, *Cantina Cuatro Cañas,* I would have literally lost my tongue sooner than later.

This electronic contraption that for twenty Mexican cents would play anyone's favorite song fascinated me. With five twenty-Mexican-cent coins—one peso—my brother had estimated that we could listen to the *same* song five consecutive times, a pleasure our old Motorola radio could never provide.

My mother had warned that women—including little girls—were forbidden from going into establishments such as the *Cuatro Cañas* and that terrible things would befall any woman who did. So I did not dare go inside the bar. But my mother's warning made no mention of boys. I had noticed that boys could run around without t-shirts. They didn't have to hide behind a tree or a car when they peed. It then stood to reason—to my almost-four-year-old's reason anyway—that boys were again the exception to the rule and that my brother Víctor could safely go into the cantina without any fear of being punished.

At every opportunity, my brother and I asked my mother for twenty cents to buy candy. Then Víctor went into the bar and played *"Amorcito Corazón,"* a ballad sung by the trío Los Panchos I particularly enjoyed. Afterwards, he joined me outside the bar to listen or sing along.

As expected, my mother caught us outside the *Cantina Cuatro Cañas* one day and forbade us both from going near the establishment again. To make up for our loss, my father offered to sing that tune to us at bedtime as often as he could. As time went by, he added other ballads to his nightly repertoire.

Italian songs, Spanish ballads and *pasodobles* (bullfight songs), tropical tunes, Argentinian tangoes and *milongas,* Mexican *rancheras* and *corridos,* Peruvian waltzes, Caribbean rhythms, and many other types of music found their way to my bedside, weaving the fabric of my dreams with threads of woe and joy and sorrow in lands faraway. And

I began to fantasize about the day I too could be consumed by my love for a matador in Madrid or Sevilla, or in some other exotic, distant land, and lose my heart to a wild and passionate man.

In some haphazard way, I suppose, I have fulfilled some of the romantic dreams I had then. I have never set foot in Madrid or Sevilla. But when I was twelve, while listening to his life story on the radio, I fell in love with the matador Manuel Rodríguez, "Manolete." And although I have never been to Lima or Buenos Aires, I lost a chunk of my heart and suffered the slings and arrows of political and romantic misfortune in that far out, exotic land called Berkeley, California.

Despite the two-year difference between us, Víctor and I were inseparable, but he was already six years old and he had to begin school. Although in time his willingness to have me as a constant companion would change, that winter, despite promises and threats, Víctor refused to start school without me. I was four years old. The only way I could attend school was by permission from the principal and the first-grade teacher.

Whenever people became too nosy about each other's private affairs, my mother was fond of saying that a small town can be a big hell. But one of the advantages of living in a "small big hell" is precisely that people know one another well. In my case, this proved to be a blessing since my father and mother knew Professor Martínez, the school's principal, well. My father took Víctor and me to see Professor Martínez.

"Víctor refuses to come to school without his sister," my father said to the principal. "Would it be all right if she comes with him?" he asked. "Just for a while," he added to reassure his friend that the arrangement was only temporary.

"I'll talk to Víctor's teacher and explain. I'm sure she'll agree, as long as your daughter is quiet and stays out of the way," the principal said. "As a matter of fact, we can put an extra desk for her in the back of the room. But you understand," he warned, "that even if she stays the whole year she will have to start the first grade when she finally reaches the legal age to attend."

"Understood," my father said.

Once Víctor and I knew that we would be able to attend school together, we began to wander around the building and grounds while the adults finished their conversation.

A prominent family in town had headed the fundraising efforts of a group of citizens—my father among them—to build this new school. Proudly, everyone pointed out that, unlike the old school, this new site had a separate classroom for each grade.

I liked the new school's shiny tile floors and the smell of fresh paint. But I had also liked the "old" school in the Pulido sisters' backyard, where for years children six to twelve had received individualized and group instruction under the canopy of two enormous mango trees.

I had been to that outdoor school one time with my mother. I was fascinated and amused, for the mango trees were also home to a family of parrots the Pulido sisters had not been able to chase away.

In those days, the academic year ran from February to November. The birds were gone most of the day, except during the mango season—May, June, and July—when they were joined by their feathered relatives and friends to feast at home. The parrots provided an alternate chorus to the children's daily recitations, managing finally to drive the two elderly teachers into hysterics and forcing them to push for relocation of the school.

Two days after my father talked to Professor Martínez, Víctor and I began school. As Professor Martínez had told my father, I was given a desk in the back of the classroom. I liked sitting in a corner, with a commanding view of the street and the room, intrigued and amused by all the goings-on inside and outside and thoroughly fascinated with the subjects we studied. During the next two hundred school days, I sat in my little corner quietly content. Quietly also, I learned to read and write, to add and subtract, to tell fruit from flower, clock from calendar, caterpillar from worm, dolphin from shark.

Only a few months before, my tongue had eagerly enjoyed the ripeness and texture of forbidden words. Now, like a first child in paradise, I filled my mouth with the names of animals and plants that flourished in faraway lands, as I learned about the ethereal grace of epiphytic orchids, the majestic but awesome presence of tigers in the nights of the planet, the power of the collective in the works of bees.

"They're beautiful, aren't they?" Professor Martínez said to me one time he found me looking at a book on insects. "The world really belongs to you—the children—and to the insects," he added.

At an intuitive level, I understood what he meant, for I had already been aware of the work of army ants, had witnessed the birth of hundreds of butterflies, had followed the luminous path of myriad fireflies soaring a few feet from the ground, like a restless reflection of the Milky Way. I had heard the song of the cicadas all day long and the chorus of the crickets in the evening that provided background music to my grandmother's tales of buried treasures and the ghosts who guarded them.

Sitting in that back corner of the classroom, I also glimpsed the terrible suffering people can inflict on one another, as I watched Moni, a girl who had befriended me from the start, grow more depressed each day while the bruises in her arms got larger, darker, and more frequent. One day Moni didn't come back to school, and I cried when my mother told me that my classmate was dead. What my mother didn't tell me for many years was that Moni had been killed by her own drunken father, who had caught her by the arm and thrown her against the wall.

Although my first academic year ended on such sad note, I was looking forward to the end-of-the year festivities. Naively, I asked if I could participate in the cultural program or if my drawings could be included in the students' art exhibit, but I was refused. Everyone liked me and the teachers admired my tenacity and constancy, but I wasn't even a name or a file number on the school roster. I was four, free to come to school or stay at home, but I was also an illegal student. I was invisible.

The next year, nonetheless, no one objected to my returning to school. So my brother and I started the second grade.

At the end of that second academic year, everyone was pleased that I would legally be attending school the following February.

For two years, my father had been correcting and helping me with my homework. More than anyone else he knew how well I had learned my first- and second-grade subjects, so he asked the principal to let me go on

to the third grade instead. Professor Martínez agreed.
After obtaining the consensus of the faculty, he wrote to
the state department of education asking for an exception
in my case.

Like most government offices in the world, the department was notoriously slow, so the principal was surprised—unpleasantly—when he received a prompt reply.
Not only was his request for my promotion to the third
grade denied, but he was also admonished for having allowed a four-year-old to attend school.

Trying to remain calm, my father informed me that I
had to repeat the first and second grades. I suppose my father expected me to be upset about it, but when I showed
no displeasure, he was intrigued. "Doesn't this make you
unhappy?" he asked.

"No," I replied. "It's all right. I can work on the pro-
jects I couldn't do when I was going with Víctor."

"Won't that be boring for you?"

"No," I reassured him. My father, however, looked
disappointed, so I hastily added, "But I'll go to the third
grade if you want me to."

He laughed. But a week later, he started his own campaign, aided by Professor Martínez and backed by six
teachers, the school's custodian, and some other parents
who were in favor of my promotion to the third grade.
Very soon, my defense committee—small but deter-
mined—was waging epistolary and telegraphic war
against the state department of education.

Two weeks before school started the principal received word that I was to take the final exams for all subjects in the first and second grade. If I passed them with a
ninety percent accuracy, they would consider the possi-
bility of placing me in the second grade, but *never!* in the

third grade. "That," they wrote, "would set a most undesirable precedent."

Teachers complained about the unfairness of the decision, but the department's attitude was one of take-it-or-leave-it. Since there seemed to be no choice, I was given the tests, which I passed with only occasional mistakes, as everyone expected.

On the first school day in February 1952, my father and I walked into the second-grade classroom. The teacher showed me to a student desk in the front row, close to her desk. But I wasn't happy there, and I got her permission to sit at my usual place in the remote corner of the classroom.

Because I already knew the subjects well, I was often asked to tutor other students. The following year, trying to keep me challenged, my third-grade teacher, *la maestra Diana,* began to instruct me in the recitation of poetry. She taught me how to deliver an impeccable line by sensing the rhythm of the poem, in the same way my piano teacher later helped me to understand musical phrasing. *La maestra Diana* also showed me how to use voice modulation and gestures to keep the poem alive for the listener.

When she felt satisfied with my rhetorical skills, teacher Diana asked me to memorize patriotic poems and to recite them before an audience during national holidays. My father was thrilled to have me perform, but he objected to my learning only patriotic poems. So he asked my teacher to teach me other kinds of poetry.

During the school's celebration of Mother's Day that year, I recited a poem about a young boy whose mother had died. As always, afraid that people would notice my trembling hands, I kept them laced on my chest as I recited the poem, and I concentrated on delivering my lines correctly. Little by little I began to experience the intensity of the feelings in the poem, to feel the pain of that orphan boy as if I'd been the one to lose my mother.

At some point I was aware of the unusual silence in the audience. Perhaps they were not enjoying the poem, because I wasn't using hand gestures to keep the poem "alive" for them, I thought. Still, I kept my hands laced over my chest until I delivered the last line. Then, I really looked at people. They were staring at me with teary eyes. Suddenly, they began to clap harder and harder.

Overwhelmed by the audience's enthusiastic response and the intense feelings in the poem, I ran to my father and took refuge in his arms.

Many years later, I wrote poems of my own. When asked if the poems talk about my own experience, I have only been able to answer with generalities, for in the end the only important truth is that words have the power to communicate the ineffable and that as a poet I am the language power broker. Nonetheless, every time I write a poem I wonder what it will cost me, as I remember the deceptively sweet but caustic sensation of soap on my tongue—the price I once paid for the use of such power.

TERESINKA PEREIRA
Translated by Robert Lima

*A*long
*M*y
*P*aths

The plains glisten
strung together by Texaco signs.
The road is a viper
which devours time
and fattens itself on one's hunger.

Next to me a boy dreams
while looking at distant cows
which were stars extinguished
by the color of the sun.

I am here
"a stranger as in any place."
Gas City, another Texaco,
a tree become an island
like me, suffering the spleen of afternoon.

The boy looks at me from his olive eyes
and I realize he's not a gringo either.
He senses me from his violet skin
and then I see myself transformed
readily into a cow on the sad plains.

NICOLE POLLENTIER

Ryan, Thanks for the Offer

so you're one of those that eat god for breakfast

JACK SPICER

boy with wedgwood eyes
tried other things
tied crystals to his forehead
gave blessings to
ambulances
partook of the holy bread at breakfast
lunch and dinner
bowed down at three
but no he said
his baggy jeans his tambourine
god left hollywood
and took to the streets

hangs in back alleys
waiting for the fishbones to emerge
talks to mice in the subway
rides the red line all day
for the thrill
he's crazy
pretty as the boy with the wedgwood eyes
who found him
stapled
to a telephone pole
titled lost
titled found
on a street corner
mass-produced in the trial size
papered with
catchy phrases
adopted by airport enthusiasts
worldwide
wedgwood eyes baggy jeans tambourine
boy found god
went looking
hands out his story
for free

JULIA ALVAREZ

The Kiss

EVEN AFTER they'd been married and had their
own families and often couldn't make it for other
occasions, the four daughters always came home for their
father's birthday. They would gather without husbands,
would-be husbands, or bring-home work. For this too
was part of the tradition: the daughters came home alone.
The apartment was too small for everyone, the father argued. Surely their husbands could spare them for one
overnight?

The husbands would just as soon have not gone to
their in-laws, but they felt annoyed at the father's strut-
ting. "When's he going to realize you've grown up? You
sleep with us!"

"He's almost seventy, for God's sake!" the daughters
said, defending the father. They were passionate women,
but their devotions were like roots; they were sunk into
the past towards the old man.

So for one night every November the daughters turned
back into their father's girls. In the cramped living room,

surrounded by the dark oversized furniture from the old house they grew up in, they were children again in a smaller, simpler version of the world. There was the prodigal scene at the door. The father opened his arms wide and welcomed them in his broken English: "This is your home, and never you should forget it." Inside, the mother fussed at them—their sloppy clothes; their long, loose hair; their looking tired, too skinny, too made up, and so on.

After a few glasses of wine, the father started in on what should be done if he did not live to see his next birthday. "Come on, Papi," his daughters coaxed him, as if it were a modesty of his to perish, and they had to talk him into staying alive. After his cake and candles, the father distributed bulky envelopes that felt as if they were padded, and they were, no less than several hundreds in bills, tens and twenties and fives, all arranged to face the same way, the top one signed with the father's name, branding them his. Why not checks? the daughters would wonder later, gossiping together in the bedroom, counting their money to make sure the father wasn't playing favorites. Was there some illegality that the father stashed such sums away? Was he—none of the daughters really believed this, but to contemplate it was a wonderful little explosion in their heads—was he maybe dealing drugs or doing abortions in his office?

At the table there was always the pretense of trying to give the envelopes back. "No, no, Papi, it's your birthday after all."

The father told them there was plenty more where that had come from. The revolution in the old country had failed. Most of his comrades had been killed or bought off. He had escaped to this country. And now it was every man for himself, so what he made was for his girls. The father never gave his daughters money when their husbands were around. "They might receive the wrong idea," the father once said, and although none of the daughters knew specifically what the father meant, they all understood what he was saying to them: Don't bring the men home for my birthday.

But this year, for his seventieth birthday, the youngest daughter, Sofía, wanted the celebration at her house. Her son had been born that summer, and she did not want to be traveling in November with a four-month-old and her little girl. And yet, she, of all the daughters, did not want to be the absent one because for the first time since she'd run off with her husband six years ago, she and her father were on speaking terms. In fact, the old man had been out to see her—or really to see his grandson—twice. It was a big deal that Sofía had had a son. He was the first male born into the family in two generations. In fact, the baby was to be named for the grandfather—Carlos—and his middle name was to be Sofía's maiden name, and so, what the old man had never hoped for with his "harem of four girls," as he liked to joke, his own name was to be kept going in this new country!

During his two visits, the grandfather had stood guard by the crib all day, speaking to little Carlos. "Charles the Fifth; Charles Dickens; Prince Charles." He enumerated the names of famous Charleses in order to stir up genetic ambition in the boy. "Charlemagne," he cooed at him also, for the baby was large and big-boned with blond fuzz on his pale pink skin and blue eyes just like his German father's. All the grandfather's Caribbean fondness for a male heir and for fair Nordic looks had surfaced. There was now good blood in the family against a future bad choice by one of its women.

"You can be president, you were born here," the grandfather crooned. "You can go to the moon, maybe even to Mars by the time you are of my age."

His macho baby talk brought back Sofía's old antagonism towards her father. How obnoxious for him to go on and on like that while beside him stood his little granddaughter, wide eyed and sad at all the things her baby brother, no bigger than one of her dolls, was going to be able to do just because he was a boy. "Make him stop, please," Sofía asked her husband. Otto was considered the jolly, good-natured one among the brothers-in-law. "The camp counselor," his sisters-in-law teased. Otto approached the grandfather. Both men looked fondly down at the new Viking.

"You can be as great a man as your father," the grandfather said. This was the first compliment the father-in-law had ever paid any son-in-law in the family. There was no way Otto was going to mess with the old man now. "He is a good boy, is he not, Papi?" Otto's German accent thickened with affection. He clapped his hand on his father-in-law's shoulders. They were friends now.

But though the father had made up with his son-in-law, there was still a strain with his own daughter. When he had come to visit, she embraced him at the door, but he stiffened and politely shrugged her off. "Let me put down these heavy bags, Sofía." He had never called her by her family pet name, Fifi, even when she lived at home. He had always had problems with his maverick youngest, and her running off hadn't helped. "I don't want loose women in my family," he had cautioned all his daughters. Warnings were delivered communally, for even though there was usually the offending daughter of the moment, every woman's character could use extra scolding.

His daughters had had to put up with this kind of attitude in an unsympathetic era. They grew up in the late sixties. Those were the days when wearing jeans and hoop earrings, smoking a little dope, and sleeping with their classmates were considered political acts against the military-industrial complex. But standing up to their father was a different matter altogether. Even as grown women, they lowered their voices in their father's earshot when alluding to their bodies' pleasure. Professional women, too, all three of them, with degrees on the wall!

Sofía was the one without the degrees. She had always gone her own way, though she downplayed her choices, calling them accidents. Among the four sisters, she was considered the plain one, with her tall, big-boned body and large-featured face. And yet, she was the one with "nonstop boyfriends," her sisters joked, not without wonder and a little envy. They admired her and were always asking her advice about men. The third daughter had shared a room with Sofía growing up. She liked to watch her sister move about their room, getting ready for bed, brushing and arranging her hair in a clip before easing herself under the sheets as if someone were waiting for her there. In the dark, Fifi gave off a fresh, wholesome smell of clean flesh. It gave solace to the third daughter, who was always so tentative and terrified and had such troubles with men. Her sister's breathing in the dark room was like having a powerful, tamed animal at the foot of her bed ready to protect her.

The youngest daughter had been the first to leave home. She had dropped out of college, in love. She had taken a job as a secretary and was living at home because her father had threatened to disown her if she moved out on her own. On her vacation she went to Colombia because her current boyfriend was going, and since she couldn't spend an overnight with him in New York, she had to travel thousands of miles to sleep with him. In Bogotá, they discovered that once they could enjoy the forbidden fruit, they lost their appetite. They broke up. She met a tourist on the street, some guy from Germany, just like that. The woman had not been without a boyfriend for more than a few days of her adult life. They fell in love.

On her way home, she tossed her diaphragm in the first bin at Kennedy Airport. She was taking no chances. But the father could tell. For months, he kept an eye out. First chance he got, he went through her drawers "looking for my nail clippers," and there he found her packet of love letters. The German man's small, correct handwriting mentioned unmentionable things—bed conversations were recreated on the thin blue sheets of aerogramme letters.

"What is the meaning of this?" The father shook the letters in her face. They had been sitting around the table, the four sisters, gabbing, and the father had come in, beating the packet against his leg like a whip, the satin hair ribbon unraveling where he had untied it, and then wrapped it round and round in a mad effort to contain his youngest daughter's misbehavior.

"Give me those!" she cried, lunging at him.

The father raised his hand with the letters above both their heads like the Statue of Liberty with her freedom torch, but he had forgotten this was the daughter who was as tall as he was. She clawed his arm down and clutched the letters to herself as if they were her baby he'd plucked from her breast. It seemed a biological rather than a romantic fury.

After his initial shock, the father regained his own

fury. "Has he deflowered you? That's what I want to know. Have you gone behind the palm trees? Are you dragging my good name through the dirt, that is what I would like to know!" The father was screaming crazily in the youngest daughter's face, question after question, not giving the daughter a chance to answer. His face grew red with fury, but hers was more terrible in its impassivity, a pale ivory moon, pulling and pulling at the tide of his anger, until it seemed he might drown in his own outpouring of fury.

Her worried sisters stood up, one at each arm, coaxing him like nurses, another touching the small of his back as if he were a feverish boy. "Come on, Papi, simmer down now. Take it easy. Let's talk. We're a family, after all."

"Are you a whore?" the father interrogated his daughter. There was spit on the daughter's cheeks from the closeness of his mouth to her face.

"It's none of your fucking business!" she said in a low, ugly-sounding voice like the snarl of an animal who could hurt him. "You have no right, no right at all, to go through my stuff or read my mail!" Tears spurted out of her eyes, her nostrils flared.

The father's mouth opened in a little zero of shock. Quietly, Sofía drew herself up and left the room. Usually, in her growing-up tantrums, this daughter would storm out of the house and come back hours later, placated, the sweetness in her nature reasserted, bearing silly gifts for everyone in the family, refrigerator magnets, little stuffed hairballs with roll-around eye-balls.

But this time they could hear her upstairs, opening and closing her drawers, moving back and forth from the bed to the closet. Downstairs, the father prowled up and down the length of the rooms, his three daughters caging him while the other great power in the house, tidily—as if she had all the time in the world—buttoned and folded all her clothes, packed all her bags, and left the house forever. She got herself to Germany somehow and got the man to marry her. To throw in the face of the father who was so ambitious for presidents and geniuses in the family, the German nobody turned out to be a world-class chemist. But the daughter's was not a petty nature. What did she care what Otto did for a living when she had shown up at his door and offered herself to him.

"I can love you as much as anybody else," she said. "If you can do the same for me, let's get married."

"Come on in and let's talk," Otto had said, or so the story went.

"Yes or no," Sofía answered. Just like that on a snowy night someone at his door and a cold draft coming in. "I couldn't let her freeze," Otto boasted later.

"Like hell you couldn't!" Sofía planted a large hand on his shoulder, and anyone could see how it must be between them in the darkness of their lovemaking. On their honeymoon, they traveled to Greece, and Sofía sent her mother and father and sisters postcards like any newlywed. "We're having a great time. Wish you were here."

But the father kept to his revenge. For months no one could mention the daughter's name in his presence, though he kept calling them all "Sofía" and quickly correcting himself. When the daughter's baby girl was born, his wife put her foot down. Let him carry his grudge to the grave, *she* was going out to Michigan (where Otto had relocated) to see her first grandchild!

Last minute, the father relented and went along, but he might as well have stayed away. He was grim and

silent the whole visit, no matter how hard Sofía and her
sisters tried to engage him in conversation. Banishment
was better than this cold shoulder. But Sofía tried again.
On the old man's next birthday, she appeared at the
apartment with her little girl. "Surprise!" There was a
reconciliation of sorts. The father first tried to shake
hands with her. Thwarted, he then embraced her stiffly
before taking the baby in his arms under the watchful eye
of his wife. Every year after that, the daughter came for
her father's birthday, and in the way of women, soothed
and stitched and patched over the hurt feelings. But there
it was under the social fabric, the raw wound. The father
refused to set foot in the daughter's house. They rarely
spoke; the father said public things to her in the same
tone of voice he used with his sons-in-law.

But now his seventieth birthday was coming up, and
he had agreed to have the celebration at Sofía's house. The
christening for little Carlos was scheduled for the morning, so the big event would be Papi Carlos's party that
night. It was a coup for the youngest daughter to have
gathered the scattered family in the Midwest for a weekend. But the real coup was how Sofía had managed to
have the husbands included this year. The husbands are
coming, the husbands are coming, the sisters joked. Sofía
passed the compliment off on little Carlos. The boy had
opened the door for the other men in the family.

But the coup the youngest daughter most wanted was
to reconcile with her father in a big way. She would throw
the old man a party he wouldn't forget. For weeks she
planned what they would eat, where they would all sleep,
the entertainment. She kept calling up her sisters with
every little thing to see what they thought. Mostly, they
agreed with her: a band, paper hats, balloons, buttons

that broadcast THE WORLD'S GREATEST DAD. Everything overdone and silly and devoted the way they knew the father would like it. Sofía briefly considered a belly dancer or a girl who'd pop out of a cake. But the third daughter, who had become a feminist in the wake of her divorce, said she considered such locker-room entertainments offensive. A band with music was what she'd pitch in on; her married sisters could split it three ways if they wanted to be sexists. With great patience, Sofía created a weekend that would offend no one. They were going to have a good time in her house for the old man's seventieth, if it killed her!

The night of the party, the family ate an early dinner before the band and the guests arrived. Each daughter toasted both Carloses. The sons-in-law called big Carlos, "Papi." Little Carlos, looking very much like a little girl in his long, white christening gown, bawled the whole time, and his poor mother had not a moment's peace between serving the dinner she'd prepared for the family and giving him his. The phone kept ringing, relatives from the old country calling with congratulations for the old man. The toasts the daughters had prepared kept getting interrupted. Even so, their father's eyes glazed with tears more than once as the four girls went through their paces.

He looked old tonight, every single one of his seventy years was showing. Perhaps it was that too much wine had darkened his complexion, and his white hair and brows and mustache stood out unnaturally white. He perked up a little for his gifts, though, gadgets and books and desk trophies from his daughters and cards with long notes penned inside "to the best, dearest Papi in the world," each one of which the old man wanted to read out loud. "No you don't, Papi, they're private!" his daughters chimed in, crowding around him, wanting to spare each other the embarrassment of having their gushing made public. His wife gave him a gold watch. The third daughter teased that that's how companies retired their employees, but when her mother made angry eyes at her, she stopped. Then there were the men gifts—belts and credit card wallets from the sons-in-law.

"Things I really need." The father was gracious. He stacked up the gift cards and put them away in his pocket to pore over later. The sons-in-law all knew that the father was watching them, jealously, for signs of indifference or self-interest. As for his girls, even after their toasts were given, the gifts opened, and the father had borne them out of the way with the help of his little granddaughter, even then, the daughters felt that there was something else he had been waiting for which they had not yet given him.

But there was still plenty of party left to make sure he got whatever it was he needed for the long, lonely year ahead. The band arrived, three middle-aged men, each with a silver wave slicked back with too much hair cream. DANNY AND HIS BOYS set up a placard with their name against the fireplace. There was one on an accordion, another on a fiddle, and a third was miscellaneous on maracas and triangle and drums when needed. They played movie themes, polkas, anything familiar you could hum along to; the corny songs were all dedicated to "Poppy" or "his lovely lady." The father liked the band. "Nice choice," he congratulated Otto. The youngest daughter's temper flared easily with all she'd had to drink and eat. She narrowed her eyes at her smiling husband and put a hand on her hip. As if Otto had lifted a finger during her long months of planning!

The guests began to arrive, many with tales of how they'd gotten lost on the way; the suburbs were dark and intricate like mazes with their courts and cul-de-sacs. Otto's unmarried colleagues looked around the room, trying to single out the recently divorced sister they'd heard so much about. But there was no one as beautiful and funny and talented as Sofía had boasted the third oldest would be. Most of these friends were half in love with Sofía anyway, and it was she they sought out in the crowded room.

There was a big chocolate cake in the shape of a heart set out on the long buffet with seventy-one candles—one for good luck. The granddaughter and her aunts had counted them and planted them diagonally across the heart, joke candles that wouldn't blow out. Later, they burned a flaming arrow that would not quit. The bar was next to the heart and by midnight when the band broke out again with "Happy Birthday, Poppy," everyone had had too much to eat and drink.

They'd been playing party games on and off all night. The band obliged with musical chairs, but after two of the dining room chairs were broken, they left off playing. The third daughter, especially, had gotten out of hand, making musical chairs of every man's lap. The father sat without speaking. He gazed upon the scene disapprovingly.

In fact, the older the evening got, the more withdrawn the father had become. Surrounded by his daughters and their husbands and fancy, intelligent, high-talking friends, he seemed to be realizing that he was just an old man sitting in their houses, eating up their roast lamb, impinging upon their lives. The daughters could almost hear his thoughts inside their own heads. He, who had paid to straighten their teeth and smooth the accent out of their English in expensive schools, he was nothing to them now. Everyone in this room would survive him, even the silly men in the band who seemed like boys—imagine making a living out of playing birthday songs! How could they ever earn enough money to give their daughters pretty clothes and send them to Europe during the summers so they wouldn't get bored? Where were the world's men anymore? Every last one of his sons-in-law was a kid; he could see that clearly. Even Otto, the famous scientist, was a school-boy with a pencil, doing his long division. The new son-in-law he even felt sorry for—he could see this husband would give out on his strong-willed second daughter. Already she had him giving her backrubs and going for cigarettes in the middle of the night. But he needn't worry about his girls. Or his wife, for that matter. There she sat, pretty and slim as a girl, smiling coyly at everyone when a song was dedicated to her. Eight, maybe nine, months he gave her of widowhood, and then she'd find someone to grow old with on his life insurance.

The third daughter thought of a party game to draw her father out. She took one of the baby's soft receiving blankets, blind-folded her father, and led him to a chair at the center of the room. The women clapped. The men sat down. The father pretended he didn't understand what all his daughters were up to. "How does one play this game, Mami?"

"You're on your own, Dad," the mother said, laughing. She was the only one in the family who called him by his American name.

"Are you ready, Papi?" the oldest asked.

"I am perfect ready," he replied in his heavy accent.

"Okay, now, guess who this is," the oldest said. She always took charge. This is how they worked things among the daughters.

The father nodded, his eyebrows shot up. He held on to his chair, excited, a little scared, like a boy about to be asked a hard question he knows the answer to.

The oldest daughter motioned to the third daughter, who tiptoed into the circle the women had made around the old man. She gave him a daughterly peck on the cheek.

"Who was that, Papi?" the oldest asked.

He was giggling with pleasure and could not get the words out at first. He had had too much to drink. "That was Mami," he said in a coy little voice.

"No! Wrong!" all the women cried out.

"Carla?" he guessed the oldest. He was going down the line. "Wrong!" More shouts.

"Sandi? Yoyo?"

"You guessed it," his third oldest said.

The women clapped; some bent over in hilarious laughter. Everyone had had too much to drink. And the old man was having his good time too.

"Okay, here's another coming at you." The eldest took up the game again. She put her index finger to her lips, gave everyone a meaningful glance, quietly circled the old man, and kissed him from behind on top of his head. Then she tiptoed back to where she had been standing when she had first spoken. "Who was that, Papi?" she asked, extra innocent.

"Mami?" His voice rode up, exposed and vulnerable. Then it sank back into its certainties. "That was Mami."

"Count me out," his wife said from the couch where she'd finally given in to exhaustion.

The father never guessed any of the other women in the room. That would have been disrespectful. Besides, their strange-sounding American names were hard to remember and difficult to pronounce. Still he got the benefit of their kisses under cover of his daughters. Down the line, the father went each time: "Carla?" "Sandi?" "Yoyo?" Sometimes, he altered the order, put the third daughter first or the oldest one second.

Sofía had been in the bedroom, tending to her son, who was wild with all the noise in the house tonight. She came back into the living room, buttoning her dress front, and happened upon the game. "Ooh." She rolled her eyes. "It's getting raunchy in here, ha!" She worked her hips in a mock rotation, and the men all laughed. She thrust her girlfriends into the circle and whispered to her little girl to plant the next kiss on her grandfather's nose. The women all pecked and puckered at the old man's face. The second daughter sat briefly on his lap and clucked him under the chin. Every time the father took a wrong guess, the youngest daughter laughed loudly. But soon, she noticed that he never guessed her name. After all her hard work, she was not to be included in his daughter count. Damn him! She'd take her turn and make him know it was her!

Quickly, she swooped into the circle and gave the old man a wet, open-mouthed kiss in his ear. She ran her tongue in the whorls of his ear and nibbled the tip. Then she moved back.

"Oh la la," the oldest said, laughing. "Who was that, Papi?"

The old man did not answer. The smile that had played on his lips throughout the game was gone. He sat up, alert. There was a long pause, everyone leaned forward, waiting for the father to begin with his usual, "Mami?"

But the father did not guess his wife's name. He tore at his blindfold as if it were a contagious body whose disease he might catch. The receiving blanket fell in a soft heap beside his chair. His face had darkened with shame at having his pleasure aroused in public by one of his daughters. He looked from one to the other. His gaze faltered. On the face of his youngest was the brilliant, impassive look he remembered from when she had snatched her love letters out of his hands.

"That's enough of that," he commanded in a low, furious voice. And sure enough, his party was over.

LORNA DEE CERVANTES

Bananas

for Indrek

I

In Estonia, Indrek is taking his children
to the Dollar Market to look at bananas.
He wants them to know about the presence of fruit,
about globes of light tart to the tongue, about the
twang of tangelos, the cloth of persimmons,
the dull little mons of kiwi. There is not a chance
for a taste. Where rubles are scarce, dollars are harder.
Even beef is doled out welfare-thin on Saturday's platter.
They light the few candles not reserved for the dead
and try not to think of small bites in the coming winter,
of irradiated fields or the diminished catch in the fisherman's
net. They tell of bananas yellow as daffodils. And mango—
which tastes as if the whole world came out from her womb.

I I

Columbia, 1928, bananas rot in the fields.
A strip of lost villages between railyard
and cemetery. The United Fruit Company train,
a yellow painted slug, eats up the swamps and jungle.
Campesinos replace Indians who are a dream
and a rubble of bloody stones hacked into coffins:
malaria, tuberculosis, cholera, machetes of the jefes.
They become like the empty carts that shatter
the landscape. Their hands, no longer pulling the teats
from the trees, now twist into death, into silence
and obedience. They wait in Aracataca, poised as
statues between hemispheres. They would rather be
tilling the plots for black beans. They would rather grow
wings and rise as *pericos—parrots, poets, clowns*—a word
which means all this and whose task is messenger from
Mítla, the underworld where the ancestors of the slain
arise with the vengeance of Tláloc. A stench permeates
the wind as bananas, black on the stumps, char
into odor. The murdered Mestizos have long been cleared
and begin their new duties as fertilizer for the plantations.
Feathers fall over the newly spaded soil: turquoise,
scarlet, azure, quetzál, and yellow litter
the graves like gold claws of bananas.

I I I

Dear I,

The 3´×6´ boxes in front of the hippie
market in Boulder are radiant with marigolds, some
with heads big as my Indian face. They signify
death to me, as it is Labor Day and already
I am making up the guest list for my *Día de los Muertos*
altár. I'll need *maravillas* so this year I plant *caléndulas*
for blooming through snow that will fall before November.
I am shopping for "no-spray" bananas. I forgo
the Dole and *Chiquita,* that name that always made me
blush for being christened with that title. But now
I am only a little small, though still brown enough
for the—*Where are you from?* Probably my ancestors
planted a placenta here as well as on my Califas coast
where alien shellfish replaced native mussels,
clams and oysters in 1886. *I'm from the 21st Century,*
I tell them, and feel rude for it—when all I desire
is bananas without pesticides. They're smaller
than plantains, which are green outside and firm
and golden when sliced. Fried in butter
they turn yellow as overripe fruit. And sweet.
I ask the produce manager how to crate and pack bananas
     to Estonia. She glares at me
suspiciously: *You can't do that. I know.*
There must be some law. You might spread
diseases. They would arrive as mush, anyway.
I am thinking of children in Estonia with
no fried *plátanos* to eat with their fish as

the Blond turns away, still without shedding
a smile at me—me, Hija del Sol, Earth's Daughter, lover
of bananas. I buy up Baltic wheat. I buy up organic
bananas, butter y canela. I ship banana bread.

I V

At Big Mountain uranium
sings through the dreams of the people.
Women dress in glowing symmetries, sheep
clouds gather below the bluffs, sundown
sandstone blooms in four corners. Smell of sage
penetrates as state tractors with chains trawl the resistant
plants, gouging anew the tribal borders, uprooting
all in their path like Amazonian ants, breaking
the hearts of the widows. Elders and children
cut the fence again and again as wind whips
the waist of ancient rock. Sheep nip across
centuries in the people's blood, and are carried
off by the Federal choppers waiting in the canyon
with orders and slings. A long winter, little wool
to spin, medicine lost in the desecration of the desert.
Old women weep as the camera rolls on the dark
side of conquest. Encounter rerun. Uranium. 1992.

V

I worry about winter in a place
I've never been, about exiles in their

homeland gathered around a fire,
about the slavery of substance and
gruel: *Will there be enough to eat?*
Will there be enough to feed? And
they dream of beaches and pies, hemispheres
of soft fruit found only in the heat of the planet.
Sugar canes, like Geiger counters, seek out tropics,
and dictate a Resolution to stun the tongues of those
who can afford to pay: imported plums, bullets,
black caviar large as peas, smoked meats
the color of Southern lynchings, what we don't
discuss in letters.
                    You are out of work.
Not many jobs today for high physicists
in Estonia, you say. *Poetry, though, is food*
for the soul. And bread? What is cake before
corn and the potato? Before the encounter
of animals, women and wheat? Stocks high
these days in survival products; 500 years later tomato
size tumors bloom in the necks of the pickers.
On my coast, Diablo dominates the golden hills,
the fault lines. On ancestral land, Vandenberg shoots nuclear
payloads to Kwajalein, a Pacific atoll, where 68% of all
infants are born amphibian or anemones. But poetry
is for the soul. I speak of spirit, the yellow seed
in air as life is the seed in water, and of the poetry
of Improbability, the magic in the Movement
of quarks and sunlight, the subtle basketry
of hadrons and neutrinos of color, how what you do
is what you get—bananas or worry.
What do you say? Your friend,
                              a Chicana poet.

SHEILA SÁNCHEZ HATCH

Sin
Palabras

W E W A L K E D D O W N Craig Street to Calav-
eras or sometimes to Navidad and continued
with no destination in mind, his six-foot-two to my
three-foot-two, hand-in-hand, *con sonrisas pero sin palabras,*
always without words. To me he was the sun smiling
down, pointing out his very own magnolias, the beauty in
mountain laurel blossoms, or maybe in a chinaberry tree.
I smiled back, held his pale, graceful fingers tinged at the
tips from rolling *cigarillos,* looking like cigarettes themselves. He wore a tan hat, like a *vaquero* because that's
what he had been, a *vaquero,* not a cowboy, on the largest
of all ranches in Texas, home of the original "big rich,"
the Kings.

Sometimes the mind machine rolls its cameras across
that ranch, years ago when he worked it, when it was still
the entire tail end of Texas. All it comes up with is a bar-
ren, dusty place: a few trees, some sort of crude mansion
in the background, and tumbleweed—thorns scraping
across the dry earth—and that's it, no more picture. So,

ashamedly, as a sort of visual aid, I'll think of *Giant*, the film with Rock Hudson, Elizabeth Taylor, and James Dean, which was supposedly based on the King family saga. I remember Sal Mineo played a Chicano going off to die in the war while his counterpart, a young Anglo played by Dennis Hopper, got to stay home. All those loosely boarded shacks that Sal and his family were forced to live in, unsanitary, nothing but brown water out of the faucets. (Which one was my grandpa's? I'd watched the movie over and over for years thinking it could help me find out.)

They come in and out of the mind program, these memories, like commercials, the only difference being that the commercial is often more important than the program. I have footage of my Abuelita, too, always with me inside, especially when I smell *cominos* or a good bowl of *caldo*. She usually does thirty-second spots in her flower-print cotton dress and white apron, rolling the perfect tortilla out on a wooden table, doing a quick three-step after spreading the dough across her hand, then dropping it flatly onto the *comal*. Smiling, with shiny black eyes, she is speaking to me, but the sound goes and there is no volume control. I couldn't hear you then and can't hear you now, grandma, say again. *Pero nada, sound's gone.*

The house on Craig Street, a small, white, wood frame house with a red brick base, was so constantly filled with the heat of family activity that even the walls would sweat, bubbling the wall paper. *Tíos, tías,* cousins, brothers, sisters, all about, and the Velásquez' home to the left was no more than ten feet away, neighbors to the right, the same. My grandmother kept a beautiful yard filled with *flores,* zinnias and tiger lilies, *matas* of all kinds on the front patio, which also held the customary swing. From the kitchen window, usually kept wide open, was a view through the greenery of mesquites and mimosa, of a bird bath in constant flow and, above and to the right, bird-feeders, always well stocked, hanging from the trees. But it's all visual with my grandparents—well, some of it is olfactory, a bit auditory, though only a couple of words, the tone or timbre of *"mijita,"* or my name called out loud.

I remember once being left in the old house alone with my *abuelos* and being frightened to death because I was only four and couldn't understand a word they said to me. I cried the whole day, terrified because my grandfather bit my cheeks, but mainly because of the unknown. The terror of those syllables falling out of their faces. I stared straight into the black caverns of their mouths, and the force of fire that came out was so totally unidentifiable that it sent lightning down my spine. I screamed and yelled and kicked and cried. I even remember standing in the doorway looking up at the lock—like the family cat needing to get outside to relieve itself. This must have been the point at which my grandpa started us walking. He always was a man of nature, and when we walked *en la brisa, todo estaba bien,* my eyes dried up and everything.

At least that is how I remember it ending happily, because honestly my memories are always incomplete, lacking real endings. I've been told they're not only incomplete but completely wrong, which could very well be true. Sometimes I create my own programs in such spectacular cinematic detail, with such memorable dialogue, that the creation no longer exists as a program but is the truth itself. There is a truth I would like to create for this story because the actual truth has gone into permanent fade-out. The control room thinks the film has melted or maybe was edited by a higher-up who believes that the viewer really doesn't need to see it or maybe the editor feels that the viewer wouldn't know how to deal with it. At any rate, the omnificent one has clipped it out, but somewhere it still lies on the cutting-room floor. Anyway, in this happy ending, the parents of the little girl child don't listen to the government, which insists that the speaking of Spanish is subversive and should be illegal. These parents don't listen, because after all, the kid must learn her language to be able to speak to her own family members. The family unit is the most important thing in life, to value it is to value the larger unit of society, no, yes? And she would like to know from her own grandfather's lips what it was like riding high in the rough, salty winds, long ago when the Kings really were kings and treated people like real peasants. The government must understand this. The government would want the kid to know her own grandfather's history, her people's history, wouldn't it? Wouldn't it? This version of the story has the kid going to school so that she wouldn't be ignorant of other cultures, other ways, so that other worlds might be opened up to them. Unfortunately, this script doesn't exactly work, the writer has no emotional distance. It must be trashed and a new writer brought in, someone not so didactic.

Okay, here it goes, totally cut and disjointed, but true to some message the mind machine wants to project, and therein is its validity. Two people, old and wrinkled worse than huge brown prunes, lie in white sheets in plain, urine-smelling rooms on metal hospital beds though not in the same hospital, in hospitals that are miles away from each other. The woman cries out for her husband, but he doesn't come. She fears he's dead, every-one around her tells her he's not dead he's just in another hospital, and then one day he is dead, dead in his bed—just a moment before he'd been crying for the sister who'd raised him. There is a little child, meanwhile, the one who stands in corners, watching, listening, but she can-not speak, cannot say one word in either language, to send him off with—only *adiós*—and goodbye would not do, would be the one thing she did not want to say. Her *abuelita* goes in much the same way, in pain, shrivelled and alone, a sorrowing soul.

Yet something happened that was not planted in the mind machine, but was a real part of the reel, in the se-quence of events that took place, this was a definite hap-pening. Just as Abuelita's soul went swirling, beginning its ascent, she saw someone or something beautiful, some-thing or someone she knew, because she smiled the most peaceful smile anyone had ever seen crease her face before. And this is where the motion picture starts, where my hope begins, the hope of Grandpa greeting her, or Christ or Buddha, maybe it was light beings or star people, but it was, and it is, and therefore she still is and he still is, and all my hope lies in the fact that when I, through with standing in corners and watching, have gotten through it all to my own ending, there they'll be, reaching for me, and in that strange space, where if there is in fact a neces-sity for words, I will say to them in words that they will understand . . .

muchas veces	i have many times
a los colibrí	fed hummingbirds
alimenté con flores	with flowers
para llevarte	to take to you

y esperé la respuesta
he visto
la mimosa de maravilla
a través de tus ojos
mi alma llenó cada árbol

habitó cada pétalo para ti
aquí traigo
un buqué de mil colores
y espero que
ahora
lo aceptes

and waited the return
i've seen
the fabulous mimosa
with your eyes
my soul filled every tree
    for you
inhabited every blossom
i have brought with me
a brightly colored bouquet
and hope that
now
you will accept it

ALMA LUZ VILLANUEVA

Dear
World,

I come to the edge of
the world at 8:10 am

to see if the tide is
high or low,

to see if the sun is
rising in winter,

to see if ducks, wild ones
still love the sky;

and the tide was high,
wild, striking cliffs

with rainbows, daily
gifts from the sun—

on the other side of
the world, people must

run in the streets, holding
their children's hands, hoping

the sniper will miss—
the old, the slow,

are killed, and no one
can touch the body

or they, too, will die—
a woman, my age, stands

on a road, her vigil, throwing
stones at trucks, full of

children, women like herself,
the old, screaming, YOU KILLED

MY BOY! YOU KILLED, YOU KILLED
MY BOY! Her boy, one year

younger than my son,
tortured, killed, made

to dig his own grave—
you see, my Earth,

I'm grateful for my life,
this magnificent world I've

come to witness—but I must
weigh her life

and mine,
daily.

SANDRA CISNEROS

Eyes
of
Zapata

I PUT MY NOSE to your eyelashes. The skin of the eyelids as soft as the skin of the penis, the collarbone with its fluted wings, the purple knot of the nipple, the dark, blue-black color of your sex, the thin legs and long thin feet. For a moment I don't want to think of your past or your future. For now you are here, you are mine.

Would it be right to tell you what I do each night you sleep here? After your cognac and cigar, after I'm certain you're asleep, I examine at my leisure your black trousers with the silver buttons—fifty-six pairs on each side; I've counted them—your embroidered sombrero with its horsehair tassel, the lovely Dutch linen shirt, the fine braid stitching on the border of your *charro* jacket, the handsome black boots, your tooled gun belt and silver spurs. Are you my general? Or only that boy I met at the country fair in San Lázaro?

Hands too pretty for a man. Elegant hands, graceful

hands, fingers smelling sweet as your Havanas. I had pretty hands once, remember? You used to say I had the prettiest hands of any woman in Cuautla. *Exquisitas* you called them, as if they were something to eat. It still makes me laugh remembering that.

Ay, but now look. Nicked and split and callused— how is it the hands get old first? The skin as coarse as the wattle of a hen. It's from the planting in the *tlacolol,* from the hard man's work I do clearing the field with the hoe and the machete, dirty work that leaves the clothes filthy, work no woman would do before the war.

But I'm not afraid of hard work or of being alone in the hills. I'm not afraid of dying or jail. I'm not afraid of the night like other women who run to the sacristy at the first call of *el gobierno.* I'm not other women.

Look at you. Snoring already? *Pobrecito.* Sleep, *papacito.* There, there. It's only me—Inés. *Duerme, mi trigueño, mi chulito, mi bebito.* Ya, ya, ya.

You say you can't sleep anywhere like you sleep here. So tired of always having to be *el gran general* Emiliano Zapata. The nervous fingers flinch, the long elegant bones shiver and twitch. Always waiting for the assassin's bullet.

Everyone is capable of becoming a traitor, and traitors must be broken, you say. A horse to be broken. A new saddle that needs breaking in. To break a spirit. Something to whip and lasso like you did in the *jaripeos* years ago.

Everything bothers you these days. Any noise, any light, even the sun. You say nothing for hours, and then when you do speak, it's an outburst, a fury. Everyone afraid of you, even your men. You hide yourself in the dark. You go days without sleep. You don't laugh anymore.

I don't need to ask; I've seen for myself. The war is not going well. I see it in your face. How it's changed over the years, Miliano. From so much watching, the face grows that way. These wrinkles new, this furrow, the jaw clenched tight. Eyes creased from learning to see in the night.

They say the widows of sailors have eyes like that, from squinting into the line where the sky and sea dissolve. It's the same with us from all this war. We're all widows. The men as well as the women, even the children. All *clinging to the tail of the horse of our* jefe *Zapata.* All of us scarred from these nine years of *aguantando*—enduring.

Yes, it's in your face. It's always been there. Since before the war. Since before I knew you. Since your birth in Anenecuilco and even before then. Something hard and tender all at once in those eyes. You knew before any of us, didn't you?

This morning the messenger arrived with the news you'd be arriving before nightfall, but I was already boiling the corn for your supper tortillas. I saw you riding in on the road from Villa de Ayala. Just as I saw you that day in Anenecuilco when the revolution had just begun and the government was everywhere looking for you. You were worried about the land titles, went back to dig them up from where you'd hidden them eighteen months earlier, under the altar in the village church—am I right?—reminding Chico Franco to keep them safe. *I'm bound to die,* you said, *someday. But our titles stand to be guaranteed.*

I wish I could rub the grief from you as if it were a smudge on the cheek. I want to gather you up in my arms as if you were Nicolás or Malena, run up to the hills. I know every cave and crevice, every back road and ravine,

but I don't know where I could hide you from yourself.
You're tired. You're sick and lonely with this war, and I
don't want any of those things to ever touch you again,
Miliano. It's enough for now you are here. For now.
Under my roof again.

Sleep, *papacito*. It's only Inés circling above you, wide-
eyed all night. The sound of my wings like the sound of a
velvet cape crumpling. A warm breeze against your skin,
the wide expanse of moon-white feathers as if I could
touch all the walls of the house at one sweep. A rustling,
then weightlessness, light scattered out the window until
it's the moist night wind beneath my owl wings. Whorl
of stars like the filigree earrings you gave me. Your tired
horse still as tin, there, where you tied it to a guamuchil
tree. River singing louder than ever since the time of the
rains.

I scout the hillsides, the mountains. My blue shadow
over the high grass and slash of *barrancas,* over the ghosts
of haciendas silent under the blue night. From this
height, the village looks the same as before the war. As if
the roofs were still intact, the walls still whitewashed, the
cobbled streets swept of rubble and weeds. Nothing blistered and burnt. Our lives smooth and whole.

Round and round the blue countryside, over the
scorched fields, giddy wind barely ruffling my stiff, white
feathers, above the two soldiers you left guarding our
door, one asleep, the other dull from a day of hard riding.
But I'm awake, I'm always awake when you are here.
Nothing escapes me. No coyote in the mountains or scorpion in the sand. Everything clear. The trail you rode
here. The night jasmine with its frothy scent of sweet
milk. The make-shift roof of cane leaves on our adobe
house. Our youngest child of five summers asleep in her

hammock—*What a little woman you are now, Malenita.*
The laughing sound of the river and canals, and the high,
melancholy voice of the wind in the branches of the tall
pine.

I slow-circle and glide into the house, bringing the
night-wind smell with me, fold myself back into my
body. I haven't left you. I don't leave you, not ever. Do
you know why? Because when you are gone I re-create
you from memory. The scent of your skin, the mole above
the broom of your mustache, how you fit in my palms.
Your skin dark and rich as *piloncillo.* This face in my
hands. I miss you. I miss you even now as you lie next to
me.

To look at you as you sleep, the color of your skin.
How in the half-light of moon you cast your own light, as
if you are all made of amber, Miliano. As if you are a little lantern, and everything in the house is golden too.

You used to be *tan chistoso. Muy bonachón, muy
bromista.* Joking and singing off-key when you had your
little drinks. *Tres vicios tengo y los tengo muy arraigados; de
ser borracho, jugador, y enamorado* . . . Ay, my life, remember? Always *muy enamorado,* no? Are you still that boy I
met at the San Lázaro country fair? Am I still that girl you
kissed under the little avocado tree? It seems so far away
from those days, Miliano.

We drag these bodies around with us, these bodies
that have nothing at all to do with you, with me, with
who we really are, these bodies that give us pleasure and
pain. Though I've learned how to abandon mine at will,
it seems to me we never free ourselves completely until
we love, when we lose ourselves inside each other. Then
we see a little of what is called heaven. When we can be
that close that we no longer are Inés and Emiliano, but

something bigger than our lives. And we can forgive, finally.

You and I, we've never been much for talking, have we? Poor thing, you don't know how to talk. Instead of talking with your lips, you put one leg around me when we sleep, to let me know it's all right. And we fall asleep like that, with one arm or a leg or one of those long monkey feet of yours touching mine. Your foot inside the hollow of my foot.

Does it surprise you I don't let go little things like that? There are so many things I don't forget even if I would do well to.

Inés, for the love I have for you. When my father pleaded, you can't imagine how I felt. How a pain entered my heart like a current of cold water and in that current were the days to come. But I said nothing.

Well then, my father said, *God help you. You've turned out just like the* perra *that bore you.* Then he turned around and I had no father.

I never felt so alone as that night. I gathered my things in my *rebozo* and ran out into the darkness to wait for you by the jacaranda tree. For a moment, all my courage left me. I wanted to turn around, call out, 'apá, beg his forgiveness, and go back to sleeping on my *petate* against the cane-rush wall, waking before dawn to prepare the corn for the day's tortillas.

Perra. That word, the way my father spat it, as if in that one word I were betraying all the love he had given me all those years, as if he were closing all the doors to his heart.

Where could I hide from my father's anger? I could put out the eyes and stop the mouths of all the saints that wagged their tongues at me, but I could not stop my heart from hearing that word—*perra.* My father, my love, who would have nothing to do with me.

You don't like me to talk about my father, do you? I know, you and he never, well . . . Remember that thick scar across his left eyebrow? Kicked by a mule when he was a boy. Yes, that's how it happened. Tía Chucha said it was the reason he sometimes acted like a mule—but you're as stubborn as he was, aren't you, and no mule kicked you.

It's true, he never liked you. Since the days you started buying and selling livestock all through the *rancheritos.* By the time you were working the stables in Mexico City there was no mentioning your name. Because you'd never slept under a thatch roof, he said. Because you were a *charro,* and didn't wear the cotton whites of the *campesino.* Then he'd mutter, loud enough for me to hear, *That one doesn't know what it is to smell his own shit.*

I always thought you and he made such perfect enemies because you were so much alike. Except, unlike you, he was useless as a soldier. I never told you how the government forced him to enlist. Up in Guanajuato is where they sent him when you were busy with the Carrancistas, and Pancho Villa's boys were giving everyone a rough time up north. My father, who'd never been farther than Amecameca, gray haired and broken as he was, they took him. It was during the time the dead were piled up on the street corners like stones, when it wasn't safe for anyone, man or woman, to go out into the streets.

There was nothing to eat, Tía Chucha sick with the fever, and me taking care of us all. My father said better he should go to his brother Fulgencio's in Tenexcapán and see if they had corn there. *Take Malenita,* I said. *With a child they won't bother you.*

And so my father went out toward Tenexcapán dragging Malenita by the hand. But when night began to fall and they hadn't come back, well, imagine. It was the widow Elpidia who knocked on our door with Malenita howling and with the story they'd taken the men to the railroad station. *South to the work camps, or north to fight?* Tía Chucha asked. *If God wishes,* I said, *he'll be safe.*

That night Tía Chucha and I dreamt this dream. My father and my Tío Fulgencio standing against the back wall of the rice mill. *Who lives?* But they don't answer, afraid to give the wrong *viva. Shoot them; discuss politics later.*

At the moment the soldiers are about to fire, an officer, an acquaintance of my father's from before the war, rides by and orders them set free.

Then they took my father and my Tío Fulgencio to the train station, shuttled them into box cars with others, and didn't let them go until they reached Guanajuato where they were each given guns and orders to shoot at the Villistas.

With the fright of the firing squad and all, my father was never the same. In Guanajuato, he had to be sent to the military hospital, where he suffered a collapsed lung. They removed three of his ribs to cure him, and when he was finally well enough to travel, they sent him back to us.

All through the dry season my father lived on like that, with a hole in the back of his chest from which he breathed. Those days I had to swab him with a sticky pitch pine and wrap him each morning in clean bandages. The opening oozed a spittle like the juice of the prickly pear, sticky and clear and with a smell both sweet and terrible like magnolia flowers rotting on the branch.

We did the best we could to nurse him, my Tía Chucha and I. Then one morning a *chachalaca* flew inside the house and battered against the ceiling. It took both of us with blankets and the broom to get it out. We didn't say anything but we thought about it for a long time.

Before the next new moon, I had a dream I was in church praying a rosary. But what I held between my hands wasn't my rosary with the glass beads, but one of human teeth. I let it drop, and the teeth bounced across the flagstones like pearls from a necklace. The dream and the bird were sign enough.

When my father called my mother's name one last time and died, the syllables came out sucked and coughed from that other mouth, like a drowned man's, and he expired finally in one last breath from that opening that killed him.

We buried him like that, with his three missing ribs wrapped in a handkerchief my mother had embroidered with his initials and with the hoofmark of the mule under his left eyebrow.

For eight days people arrived to pray the rosary. All the priests had long since fled, we had to pay a *rezandero* to say the last rites. Tía Chucha laid the cross of lime and sand, and set out flowers and a votive lamp; and on the ninth day, my *tía* raised the cross and called out my father's name—Remigio Alfaro—and my father's spirit flew away and left us.

But suppose he won't give us his permission.

That old goat, we'll be dead by the time he gives his permission. Better we just run off. He can't be angry forever.

Not even on his deathbed did he forgive you. I suppose you've never forgiven him either for calling in the authorities. I'm sure he only meant for them to scare you a little, to remind you of your obligations to me since I was expecting your child. Who could imagine they would force you to join the cavalry.

I can't make apologies on my father's behalf, but, well, what were we to think, Miliano? Those months you were gone, hiding out in Puebla because of the protest signatures, the political organizing, the work in the village defense. Me as big as a boat, Nicolás waiting to be born at any moment, and you nowhere to be found, and no money sent, and not a word. I was so young, I didn't know what else to do but abandon our house of stone and adobe and go back to my father's. Was I wrong to do that? You tell me.

I could endure my father's anger, but I was afraid for the child. I placed my hand on my belly and whispered— Child, be born when the moon is tender; even a tree must be pruned under the full moon so it will grow strong. And at the next full moon, I gave light, Tía Chucha holding up our handsome, strong-lunged boy.

Two planting seasons came and went, and we were preparing for the third when you came back from the cavalry and met your son for the first time. I thought you'd forgotten all about politics, and we could go on with our lives. But by the end of the year, you were already behind the campaign to elect Patricio Leyva governor, as if all the troubles with the government, with my father, had meant nothing.

You gave me a pair of gold earrings as a wedding gift, remember? *I never said I'd marry you, Inés. Never.* Two filagree hoops with tiny flowers and fringe. I buried them when the government came, and went back for them later. But even these I had to sell when there was nothing to eat but boiled corn silk. They were the last things I sold.

Never. It made me feel a little crazy when you hurled that at me. That word with all its force.

But, Miliano, I thought . . .

You were foolish to have thought then.

That was years ago. We're all guilty of saying things we don't mean. I *never said . . .* I know. You don't want to hear it.

What am I to you now, Miliano? When you leave me? When you hesitate? Hover? The last time you gave a sigh that would fit into a spoon. What did you mean by that?

If I complain about these woman concerns of mine, I know you'll tell me—Inés, these aren't times for that— wait until later. But, Miliano, I'm tired of being told to wait.

Ay, you don't understand. Even if you had the words, you could never tell me. You don't know your own heart, men. Even when you are speaking with it in your hand.

I have my livestock, a little money my father left me. I'll set up a house for us in Cuautla of stone and adobe. We can live to- gether, and later we'll see.

Nicholas is crazy about his two cows, La Fortuna y La Paloma. Because he's a man now, you said, when you gave him his birthday present. When you were thirteen, you were already buying and reselling animals throughout the ranches. To see if a beast is a good worker, you must tickle it on the back, no? If it can't bother itself to move, well then, it's lazy and won't be of any use. See, I've learned that much from you.

Remember the horse you found in Cuernavaca? Some- one had hidden it in an upstairs bedroom, wild and spir- ited from being penned so long. She had poked her head from between the gold fringe of velvet drapery just as you rode by, just at that moment. A beauty like that making her appearance from a balcony like a woman waiting for her serenade. You laughed and joked about that and named her La Coquetona, remember? La Coquetona, yes.

When I met you at the country fair in San Lázaro, everyone knew you were the best man with horses in the state of Morelos. All the hacienda owners wanted you to work for them. Even as far as Mexico City. A *charro* among *charros.* The livestock, the horses bought and sold. Planting a bit when things were slow. Your brother Eufemio borrowing time and time again because he'd squandered every peso of his inheritance, but you've always prided yourself in being independent, no? You once confessed one of the happiest days of your life was the watermelon harvest that produced the 600 pesos.

And *my* happiest memory? The night I came to live with you, of course. I remember how your skin smelled sweet as the rind of a watermelon, like the fields after it has rained. I wanted my life to begin there, at that moment when I balanced that thin boy's body of yours on mine, as if you were made of balsa, as if you were boat and I river. The days to come, I thought, erasing the bitter sting of my father's good-bye.

There's been too much suffering, too much of our hearts hardening and drying like corpses. We've survived, eaten grass and corn cobs and rotten vegetables. And the epidemics have been as dangerous as the *federales,* the deserters, the bandits. Nine years.

In Cuautla it stank from so many dead. Nicolás would go out to play with the bullet shells he'd collected, or to watch the dead being buried in trenches. Once five federal corpses were piled up in the *zócalo.* We went through their pockets for money, jewelry, anything we could sell.

When they burned the bodies, the fat ran off them in streams, and they jumped and wiggled as if they were trying to sit up. Nicolás had terrible dreams after that. I was too ashamed to tell him I did, too.

At first we couldn't bear to look at the bodies hanging in the trees. But after many months, you get used to them, curling and drying into leather in the sun day after day, dangling like earrings, so that they no longer terrify, they no longer mean anything. Perhaps that is worst of all.

Your sister tells me Nicolás takes after you these days, nervous and quick with words, like a sudden dust storm or shower of sparks. When you were away with the Seventh Cavalry, Tía Chucha and I would put smoke in Nicolás's mouth, so he would learn to talk early. All the other babies his age babbling like monkeys, but Nicolás always silent, always following us with those eyes all your kin have. Those are not Alfaro eyes, I remember my father saying.

The year you came back from the cavalry, you sent for us, me and the boy, and we lived in the house of stone and adobe. From your silences, I understood I was not to question our marriage. It was what it was. Nothing more. Wondering where you were the weeks I didn't see you, and why it was you arrived only for a few slender nights, always after nightfall and leaving before dawn. Our lives ran along as they had before. What good is it to have a husband and not have him? I thought.

When you began involving yourself with the Patricio Leyva campaign, we didn't see you for months at a time. Sometimes the boy and I would return to my father's house where I felt less alone. *Just for a few nights,* I said, unrolling a *petate* in my old corner against the cane-rush wall in the kitchen. *Until my husband returns.* But a few nights grew into weeks, and the weeks into months, until I spent more time under my father's thatch roof than in our house with the roof of tiles.

That's how the weeks and months passed. Your election to the town council. Your work defending the land titles. Then the parceling of the land when your name began to run all along the villages, up and down the Cuautla River. Zapata this and Zapata that. I couldn't go anywhere without hearing it. And each time, a kind of fear entered my heart like a cloud crossing the sun.

I spent the days chewing on this poison as I was grinding the corn, pretending to ignore what the other women washing at the river said. That you had several *pastimes.* That there was a certain María Josefa in Villa de Ayala. Then they would just laugh. It was worse for me those nights you did arrive and lay asleep next to me. I lay awake watching and watching you.

In the day, I could support the grief, wake up before dawn to prepare the day's tortillas, busy myself with the chores, the turkey hens, the planting and collecting of herbs. The boy already wearing his first pair of trousers and getting into all kinds of trouble when he wasn't being watched. There was enough to distract me in the day. But at night, you can't imagine.

Tía Chucha made me drink heart-flower tea—*yoloxochitl,* flower from the magnolia tree—petals soft and seamless as a tongue. *Yoloxochitl, flor de corazón,* with its breath of vanilla and honey. She prepared a tonic with the dried blossoms and applied a salve, mixed with the white of an egg, to the tender skin above my heart.

It was the season of rain. *Plum . . . plum plum.* All

night I listened to that broken string of pearls, bead upon bead upon bead rolling across the waxy leaves of my heart.

I lived with that heartsickness inside me, Miliano, as if the days to come did not exist. And when it seemed the grief would not let me go, I wrapped one of your hand-kerchiefs around a dried hummingbird, went to the river, whispered, *Virgencita, ayúdame,* kissed it, then tossed the bundle into the waters where it disappeared for a moment before floating downstream in a dizzy swirl of foam.

That night, my heart circled and fluttered against my chest, and something beneath my eyelids palpitated so furiously, it wouldn't let me sleep. When I felt myself whirling against the beams of the house, I opened my eyes. I could see perfectly in the darkness. Beneath me— all of us asleep. Myself, there, in my *petate* against the kitchen wall, the boy asleep beside me. My father and my Tía Chucha sleeping in their corner of the house. Then I felt the room circle once, twice, until I found myself under the stars flying above the little avocado tree, above the house and the corral.

I passed the night in a delirious circle of sadness, of joy, reeling round and round above our roof of dried sug-arcane leaves, the world as clear as if the noon sun shone. And when dawn arrived I flew back to my body that waited patiently for me where I'd left it, on the *petate* be-side our Nicolás.

Each evening I flew a wider circle. And in the day, I withdrew further and further into myself, living only for those night flights. My father whispered to my Tía Chucha, Ojos *que no ven, corazón que no siente.* But my eyes did see, and my heart suffered.

One night over *milpas* and beyond the *tlacolol,* over *barrancas* and thorny scrub forests, past the thatch roofs of the *jacales* and the stream where the women do the wash, beyond bright bougainvillea, high above canyons and across fields of rice and corn, I flew. The gawky stalks of banana trees swayed beneath me. I saw rivers of cold water and a river of water so bitter they say it flows from the sea. I didn't stop until I reached a grove of high laurels rustling in the center of a town square where all the whitewashed houses shone blue as abalone under the full moon. And I remember my wings were blue and soundless as the wings of a *tecolote*.

And when I alighted on the branch of a tamarind tree outside a window, I saw you sleep next to that woman from Villa de Ayala, that woman who is your wife sleeping beside you. And her skin shone blue in the moonlight and you were blue as well.

She wasn't at all like I'd imagined. I came up close and studied her hair. Nothing but an ordinary woman with her ordinary woman smell. She opened her mouth and gave a moan. And you pulled her close to you, Miliano. Then I felt a terrible grief inside me. The two of you asleep like that, your leg warm against hers, your foot inside the hollow of her foot.

They say I am the one who caused her children to die. From jealousy, from envy. What do you say? Her boy and girl both dead before they stopped sucking teat. She won't bear you any more children. But my boy, my girl are alive.

When a customer walks away after you've named your price, and then he comes back, that's when you raise your price. When you know you have what he wants. Something I learned from your horse-trading years.

You married her, that woman from Villa de Ayala,

true. But see, you came back to me. You always come back. In between and beyond the others. That's my magic. You come back to me.

You visited me again Thursday last. I yanked you from the bed of that other one. I dreamt you, and when I awoke I was sure your spirit had just fluttered from the room. I have yanked you from your sleep before—into the dream I was dreaming. Twisted you like a spiral of hair around a finger. Love, you arrived with your heart full of birds. And when you would not do my bidding and come when I commanded, I turned into the soul of a *tecolote* and kept vigil in the branches of a purple jacaranda outside your door to make sure no one would do my Miliano harm while he slept.

You sent a letter by messenger how many months afterward? On paper thin and crinkled as if it had been made with tears.

I burned copal in a clay bowl. Inhaled the smoke. Said a prayer in *mexicano* to the old gods, an Ave María in Spanish to La Virgen, and gave thanks. You were on your way home to us. The house of stone and adobe aired and swept clean, the night sweet with the scent of candles that had been burning continually since I saw you in the dream. Sometime after Nicolás had fallen asleep, the hoof beats.

A silence between us like a language. When I held you, you trembled, a tree in rain. Ay, Miliano, I remember that, and it helps the days pass without bitterness.

What did you tell her about me? *That was before I knew you, Josefa. That chapter of my life with Inés Alfaro is finished.* But I'm a story that never ends. Pull one string and the whole cloth unravels.

Just before you came for Nicolás, he fell ill with the

symptoms of the jealousy sickness, big boy that he was. But it was true, I was with child again. Malena was born without making a sound, because she remembered how she had been conceived—nights tangled around each other like smoke.

You and Villa were marching triumphantly down the streets of Mexico City, your hat filled with flowers the pretty girls tossed at you. The brim sagging under the weight like a basket.

I named our daughter after my mother. María Elena. Against my father's wishes.

You have your *pastimes.* That's how it's said, no? Your many *pastimes.* I know you take to your bed women half my age. Women the age of our Nicolás. You've left many mothers crying, as they say.

They say you have three women in Jojutla, all under one roof. And that your women treat each other with *a most extraordinary harmony, sisters in a cause who believe in the greater good of the revolution.* I say they can all go to hell, those newspaper journalists and the mothers who bore them. Did they ever ask me?

These stupid country girls, how can they resist you? The magnificent Zapata in his elegant *charro* costume, riding a splendid horse. Your wide sombrero a halo around your face. You're not a man for them; you're a legend, a myth, a god. But you are as well my husband. Albeit only sometimes.

How can a woman be happy in love? To love like this, to love as strong as we hate. That is how we are, the women of my family. We never forget a wrong. We know how to love, and we know how to hate.

I've seen your other children in the dreams. María Luisa from that Gregoria Zúñiga in Quilamula after her twin sister Luz died on you childless. Diego born in Tlatizapán of that woman who calls herself *Missus* Jorge Piñeiro. Ana María in Cuautla from that she-goat Petra Torres. Mateo, son of that nobody, Jesusa Pérez of Temilpa. All your children born with those eyes of Zapata.

I know what I know. How you sleep cradled in my arms, how you love me with a pleasure close to sobbing, how I still the trembling in your chest and hold you, hold you, until those eyes look into mine.

Your eyes. Ay! Your eyes. Eyes with teeth. Terrible as obsidian. The days to come in those eyes, *el porvenir*, the days gone by. And beneath that fierceness, something ancient and tender as rain.

Miliano, Milianito. And I sing you that song I sang Nicolás and Malenita when they were little and would not sleep.

Seasons of war, a little half-peace now and then, and then war and war again. Running up to the hills when the *federales* come, coming back down when they've gone.

Before the war, it was the *caciques* who were after the young girls and the married women. They had their hands on everything it seems—the land, law, women. Remember when they found that *desgraciado* Policarpo Cisneros in the arms of the Quintero girl? *¡Virgen purísima!* She was only a little thing of twelve years. And he, what? At least eighty, I imagine.

Desgraciados. All members of one army against us, no? The *federales,* the *caciques,* one as bad as the other, stealing our hens, stealing the women at night. What long sharp howls the women would let go when they carried them off. The next morning the women would be back, and we would say *Buenos días,* as if nothing had happened.

Since the war began, we've gotten used to sleeping in the corral. Or in the hills, in trees, in caves with the spiders and scorpions. We hide ourselves as best we can when the *federales* arrive, behind rocks or in *barrancas,* or in the pine and tall grass when there is nothing else to hide behind. Sometimes I build a shelter for us with cane branches in the mountains. Sometimes the people of the cold lands give us boiled water sweetened with cane sugar, and we stay until we can gather a little strength, until the sun has warmed our bones and it is safe to come back down.

Before the war, when Tía Chucha was alive, we passed the days selling at all the town markets—chickens, turkey hens, cloth, coffee, the herbs we collected in the hills or grew in the garden. That's how our weeks and months came and went.

I sold bread and candles. I planted corn and beans back then and harvested coffee at times too. I've sold all kinds of things. I even know how to buy and resell animals. And now I know how to work the *tlacolol,* which is the worst of all—your hands and feet split and swollen from the machete and hoe.

Sometimes I find sweet potatoes in the abandoned fields or squash, or corn. And this we eat raw, too tired, too hungry to cook anything. We've eaten like the birds, what we could pluck from the trees—guava, mango, tamarind, almond when in season. We've gone without corn for the tortillas, made do when there were no kernels to be had, eaten the cobs as well as the flower.

My *metate,* my good shawl, my fancy *huipil,* my filigree earrings, anything I could sell, I've sold. The corn sells for one peso and a half a *cuartillo* when one can find a handful. I soak and boil and grind it without even letting it cool, a few tortillas to feed Malenita, who is always hungry, and if there is anything left, I feed myself.

Tía Chucha caught the sickness of the wind in the hot country. I used all her remedies and my own, *guacamaya* feathers, eggs, cocoa beans, chamomile oil, rosemary, but there was no help for her. I thought I would finish myself crying, all my mother's people gone from me, but there was the girl to think about. Nothing to do but go on, *aguantar,* until I could let go that grief. Ay, how terrible those times.

I go on surviving, hiding, searching if only for Malenita's sake. Our little plantings, that's how we get along. The government ran off with the *maíz,* the chickens, my prize turkey hens and rabbits. Everyone has had his turn to do us harm.

Now I'm going to tell you about when they burned the house, the one you bought for us. I was sick with the fever. Headache and a terrible pain in the back of my calves. Fleas, babies crying, gunshots in the distance, someone crying out *el gobierno,* a gallop of horses in my head, and the shouting of those going off to join troops and of those staying. I could barely manage to drag myself up the hills. Malenita was suffering one of her *corajes* and refused to walk, sucking the collar of her blouse and crying. I had to carry her on my back with her little feet kicking me all the way until I gave her half of a hard tortilla to eat and she forgot about her anger and fell asleep. By the time the sun was strong and we were far away enough to feel safe, I was weak. I slept without dreaming, holding Malenita's cool body against my burning. When

I woke the world was filled with stars, and the stars carried me back to the village and showed me.

It was like this. The village did not look like our village. The trees, the mountains against the sky, the land, yes, that was still as we remembered it, but the village was no longer a village. Everything pocked and in ruins. Our house with its roof tiles gone. The walls blistered and black. Pots, pans, jugs, dishes axed into shards, our shawls and blankets torn and trampled. The seed we had left, what we'd saved and stored that year, scattered, the birds enjoying it.

Hens, cows, pigs, goats, rabbits, all slaughtered. Not even the dogs were spared and were strung from the trees. The Carrancistas destroyed everything, because, as they say, *Even the stones here are Zapatistas.* And what was not destroyed was carried off by their women, who descended behind them like a plague of vultures to pick us clean.

It's *her* fault, the villagers said when they returned. *Nagual. Bruja.* Then I understood how alone I was.

Miliano, what I'm about to say to you now, only to you do I tell it, to no one else have I confessed it. It's necessary I say it; I won't rest until I undo it from my heart.

They say when I was a child I caused a hailstorm that ruined the new corn. When I was so young I don't even remember. In Tetelcingo that's what they say.

That's why the years the harvest was bad and the times especially hard, they wanted to burn me with green wood. It was my mother they killed instead, but not with green wood. When they delivered her to our door, I cried until I finished myself crying. I was sick, sick, for several days, and they say I vomited worms, but I don't remember that. Only the terrible dreams I suffered during the fever.

My Tía Chucha cured me with branches from the pepper tree and with the broom. And for a long time afterward, my legs felt as if they were stuffed with rags, and I kept seeing little purple stars winking and whirling just out of reach.

It wasn't until I was well enough to go outside again that I noticed the crosses of pressed *pericón* flowers on all the village doorways and in the *milpa* too. From then on the villagers avoided me, as if they meant to punish me by not talking, just as they'd punished my mother with those words that thumped and thudded like the hail that killed the corn.

That's why we had to move the seven kilometers from Tetelcingo to Cuautla, as if we were from that village and not the other, and that's how it was we came to live with my Tía Chucha, little by little taking my mother's place as my teacher, and later as my father's wife.

My Tía Chucha, she was the one who taught me to use my sight, just as her mother had taught her. The women in my family, we've always had the power to see with more than our eyes. My mother, my Tía Chucha, me. Our Malenita as well.

It's only now when they murmur *bruja, nagual,* behind my back, just as they hurled those words at my mother, that I realize how alike my mother and I are. How words can hold their own magic. How a word can charm, and how a word can kill. This I've understood.

Mujeriego. I dislike the word. Why not *hombreiego?* Why not? The word loses its luster. *Hombreiega.* Is that what I am? My mother? But in the mouth of men, the word is flint-edged and heavy, makes a drum of the body, something to maim and bruise, and sometimes kill.

What is it I am to you? Sometime wife? Lover? Whore? Which? To be one is not so terrible as being all.

I've needed to hear it from you. To verify what I've always thought I knew. You'll say I've grown crazy from living on dried grass and corn silk. But I swear I've never seen more clearly than these days.

Ay, Miliano, don't you see? The wars begin here, in our hearts and in our beds. You have a daughter. How do you want her treated? Like you treated me?

All I've wanted was words, that magic to soothe me a little, what you could not give me.

The months I disappeared, I don't think you understood my reasons. I assumed I made no difference to you. Only Nicolás mattered. And that's when you took him from me.

When Nicolás lost his last milk tooth, you sent for him, left him in your sister's care. He's lived like deer in the mountains, sometimes following you, sometimes meeting you ahead of your campaigns, always within reach. I know I let him go. I agreed, yes, because a boy should be with his father, I said. But the truth is I wanted a part of me always hovering near you. How hard it must be for you to keep letting Nicolás go. And yet, he is always yours. Always.

When the *federales* captured Nicolás and took him to Tepaltzingo, you arrived with him asleep in your arms after your brother and Chico Franco rescued him. If anything happens to this child, you said, if anything . . . and started to cry. I didn't say anything, Miliano, but you can't imagine how in that instant, I wanted to be small and fit inside your heart, I wanted to belong to you like the boy, and know you loved me.

If I am a witch, then so be it, I said. And I took to eating black things—*huitlacoche* the corn mushroom, coffee, dark chiles, the bruised part of fruit, the darkest, blackest things to make me hard and strong.

You rarely talk. Your voice, Miliano, thin and light as a woman's, almost delicate. Your way of talking is sudden, quick, like water leaping. And yet I know what that voice of yours is capable of.

I remember after the massacre of Tlatizapán, 286 men and women and children slaughtered by the Carrancistas. Your thin figure, haggard and drawn, your face small and dark under your wide sombrero. I remember even your horse looked half-starved and wild that dusty, hot June day.

It was as if misery laughed at us. Even the sky was sad, the light leaden and dull, the air sticky and everything covered with flies. Women filled the streets searching among the corpses for their dead.

Everyone was tired, exhausted from running from the Carrancistas. The government had chased us almost as far as Jojutla. But you spoke in *mexicano,* you spoke to us in our language, with your heart in your hand, Miliano, which is why we listened to you. The people were tired, but they listened. Tired of surviving, of living, of enduring. Many were deserting and going back to their villages. *If you don't want to fight anymore,* you said, *we'll all go to the devil. What do you mean you are tired? When you elected me, I said I would represent you if you backed me. But now you must back me, I've kept my word. You wanted a man who wore pants, and I've been that man. And now, if you don't mean to fight, well then, there's nothing I can do.*

We were filthy, exhausted, hungry, but we followed you.

. . .

Under the little avocado tree behind my father's house is where you first kissed me. A crooked kiss, all wrong, on the side of the mouth. *You belong to me now,* you said, and I did.

The way you rode in the morning of the San Lázaro fair on a pretty horse as dark as your eyes. The sky was sorrel colored, remember? Everything swelled and smelled of rain. A cool shadow fell across the village. You were dressed all in black as is your custom. A graceful, elegant man, thin and tall.

You wore a short black linen *charro* jacket, black trousers of cashmere adorned with silver buttons, and a lavender shirt knotted at the collar with a blue silk neckerchief. Your sombrero had a horsehair braid and tassel and a border of carnations embroidered along the wide brim in gold and silver threads. You wore the sombrero set forward—not at the back of the head as others do—so it would shade those eyes of yours, those eyes that watched and waited. Even then I knew it was an animal to match mine.

Suppose my father won't let me?
We'll run off, he can't be angry for always.
Wait until the end of the harvest.
You pulled me toward you under the little avocado tree and kissed me. A kiss tasting of warm beer and whiskers. *You belong to me now.*

It was during the plum season we met. I saw you at the country fair at San Lázaro. I wore my braids up away from the neck with bright ribbons. My hair freshly washed and combed with oil prepared with the ground bone of the mamey. And the neckline of my *huipil,* a white one, I remember, showed off my neck and collarbones.

You were riding a fine horse, silver saddled with a fringe of red and black silk tassels, and your hands, beautiful hands, long and sensitive, rested lightly on the reins. I was afraid of you at first, but I didn't show it. How pretty you made your horse prance.

You circled when I tried to cross the *zócalo,* I remember. I pretended not to see you until you rode your horse in my path, and I tried to dodge one way, then the other, like a calf in a *jaripeo.* I could hear the laughter of your friends from under the shadows of the arcades. And when it was clear there was no avoiding you, I looked up at you and said, *With your permission.* You did not insist, you touched the brim of your hat, and let me go, and I heard your friend Francisco Franco, the one I would later know as Chico, say, *Small, but bigger than you, Miliano.*

So is it yes? I didn't know what to say, I was still so little, just laughed, and you kissed me like that, on my teeth.

Yes? and pressed me against the avocado tree. *No, is it?* And I said yes, then I said no, and yes, your kisses arriving in between.

Love? We don't say that word. For you it has to do with stroking with your eyes what catches your fancy, then lassoing and harnessing and corraling. Yanking home what is easy to take.

But not for me. Not from the start. You were handsome, yes, but I didn't like handsome men, thinking they could have whomever they wanted. I wanted to be, then, the one you could not have. I didn't lower my eyes like the other girls when I felt you looking at me.

I'll set up a house for us. We can live together, and later we'll see.
But suppose one day you leave me.
Never.
Wait at least until the end of the harvest.

I remember how your skin burned to the touch. How you smelled of lemongrass and smoke. I balanced that thin boy's body of yours on mine.

Something undid itself—gently, like a braid of hair unraveling. And I said, *Ay, mi chulito, mi chulito, mi chulito,* over and over.

Mornings and nights I think your scent is still in the blankets, wake remembering you are tangled somewhere between the sleeping and the waking. The scent of your skin, the mole above the broom of your thick mustache, how you fit in my hands.

Would it be right to tell you, each night you sleep here, after your cognac and cigar, when I'm certain you are finally sleeping, I sniff your skin. Your fingers sweet with the scent of tobacco. The fluted collarbones, the purple knot of the nipple, the deep, plum color of your sex, the thin legs and long, thin feet.

I examine at my leisure your black trousers with the silver buttons, the lovely shirt, the embroidered sombrero, the fine braid stitching on the border of your *charro* jacket, admire the workmanship, the spurs, leggings, the handsome black boots.

And when you are gone, I re-create you from memory. Rub warmth into your fingertips. Take that dimpled chin of yours between my teeth. All the parts are there except your belly. I want to rub my face in its color, say no, no, no. Ay. Feel its warmth from my left cheek to the right. Run my tongue from the hollow in your throat, between the smooth stones of your chest, across the trail of down below the navel, lose myself in the dark scent of your sex. To look at you as you sleep, the color of your skin. How in the half-light of moon you cast your own light, as if you are a man made of amber.

Are you my general? Or only my Milianito? I think, I don't know what you say, you don't belong to me nor to that woman from Villa de Ayala. You don't belong to anyone, no? Except the land. *La madre tierra que nos mantiene y cuida.* Every one of us.

I rise high and higher, the house shutting itself like an eye. I fly farther than I've ever flown before, farther than the clouds, farther than our Lord Sun, husband of the moon. Till all at once I look beneath me and see our lives, clear and still, far away and near.

And I see our future and our past, Miliano, one single thread already lived and nothing to be done about it. And I see the face of the man who will betray you. The place and the hour. The gift of a horse the color of gold dust. A breakfast of warm beer swirling in your belly. The hacienda gates opening. The pretty bugles doing the honors. *TirriLEE tirREE.* Bullets like a sudden shower of stones. And in that instant, a feeling of relief almost. And loneliness, just like that other loneliness of being born.

And I see my clean *huipil* and my silk Sunday shawl. My rosary placed between my hands and a palm cross that has been blessed. Eight days people arriving to pray. And on the ninth day, the cross of lime and sand raised, and my name called out—Inés Alfaro. The twisted neck of a rooster. Pork tamales wrapped in corn leaves. The masqueraders dancing, the men dressed as women, the women as men. Violins, guitars, one loud drum.

And I see other faces and other lives. My mother in a field of cempoaxúchitl flowers with a man who is not my father. Her *rebozo de bolita* spread beneath them. The smell of crushed grass and garlic. How, at a signal from her lover, the others descend. The clouds scurrying away. A machete-sharp cane stake greased with lard and driven into the earth. How the men gather my mother like a bundle of corn. Her sharp cry against the infinity of sky when the cane stake pierces her. How each waiting his turn grunts words like hail that splits open the skin, just as before they'd whispered words of love.

The star of her sex open to the sky. Clouds moving soundlessly, and the sky changing colors. Hours. Eyes still fixed on the clouds the morning they find her— braids undone, a man's sombrero tipped on her head, a cigar in her mouth, as if to say, this is what we do to women who try to act like men.

The small black bundle that is my mother delivered to my father's door. My father without a "who" or "how." He knows as well as everyone.

How the sky let go a storm of stones. The corn harvest ruined. And how we move from Tetelcingo to my Tía Chucha's in Cuautla.

And I see our children. Malenita with her twins, who will never marry, two brave *solteronas* living out their lives selling herbs in La Merced in Mexico City.

And our Nicolás, a grown man, the grief and shame

Nicolás will bring to the Zapata name when he kicks up a fuss about the parcel of land the government gives him, how it isn't enough, how it's never enough, how the son of a great man should not live like a peasant. The older Anenecuilcans shaking their heads when he sells the Zapata name to the PRI campaign.

And I see the ancient land titles the smoky morning they are drawn up in Náhuatl and recorded on tree-bark paper—*conceded to our pueblo the 25th of September of 1607 by the Viceroy of New Spain*—the land grants that prove the land has always been our land.

And I see that dappled afternoon in Anenecuilco when the government has begun to look for you. And I see you unearth the strong box buried under the main altar of the village church, and hand it to Chico Franco— *If you lose this, I'll have you dangling from the tallest tree,* compadre. *Not before they fill me with bullets,* Chico said and laughed.

And the evening, already as an old man, in the Canyon of the Wolves, Chico Franco running and running, old wolf, old cunning, the government men Nicolás sent shouting behind him, his sons Vírulo and Julián, young, crumpled on the cool courtyard tiles like bougainvillea blossoms, and how useless it all is, because the deeds are buried under the floorboards of a *pulquería* named La Providencia, and no one knowing where they are after the bullets pierce Chico's body. Nothing better or worse than before, and nothing the same or different.

And I see rivers of stars and the wide sea with its sad voice, and emerald fish fluttering on the sea bottom, glad to be themselves. And bell towers and blue forests, and a store window filled with hats. A burnt foot like the inside of a plum. A lice comb with two nits. The lace hem of a woman's dress. The violet smoke from a cigarette. A boy urinating into a tin. The milky eyes of a blind man. The chipped finger of a San Isidro statue. The tawny bellies of dark women giving life.

And more lives and more blood, those being born as well as those dying, the ones who ask questions and the ones who keep quiet, the days of grief and all the flower colors of joy.

Ay papacito, cielito de mi corazón, now the burros are complaining. The rooster beginning his cries. Morning already? Wait, I want to remember everything before you leave me.

How you looked at me in the San Lázaro plaza. How you kissed me under my father's avocado tree. Nights you loved me with a pleasure close to sobbing, how I stilled the trembling in your chest and held you, held you. Miliano, Milianito.

My sky, my life, my eyes. Let me look at you. Before you open those eyes of yours. The days to come, the days gone by. Before we go back to what we'll always be.

GLORIA VANDO

HE 2-104:
A True
Planetary Nebula
in the Making

On the universal clock, Sagan tells us,
we are only moments old. And this
new crablike discovery in Centaurus,
though older by far, is but
an adolescent going through a vital
if brief stage in the evolution
of interacting stars. I see it
starting its sidereal trek
through midlife, glowingly complex—
"a pulsating red giant" with a "small
hot companion" in tow—and think
of you and me that night in August
speeding across Texas in your red
Mustang convertible, enveloped in dust
and fumes, aiming for a motel bed,

settling instead for the backseat of the car,
arms and legs flailing in all directions,
but mostly toward heaven—and now
this cool red dude winking at me
through the centuries as if to say
I know, I know, sidling in closer
to his sidekick, shedding his garments,
shaking off dust, encircling
her small girth with a high-density
lasso of himself, high-velocity
sparks shooting from her ringed
body like crazy legs and arms until
at last, he's got his hot companion
in a classic hold and slowly,
in ecstasy, they take wing and
blaze as one across the Southern skies—
no longer crab but butterfly.

ROSARIO FERRÉ
Translated by Rosario Ferré
in collaboration with Nancy Taylor

The
Glass
Box

I'VE ALWAYS KNOWN that I, too, was one of the chosen. I've always trusted my dreams because I know that behind them lies the door to immortality. I've always trusted my hands, their power to create magic bridges with cables, with spiderwebs, with steel girders, with sticks of dynamite, with whatever comes to hand which may make better communication possible. They've been looking for me for a long time now, although so far they haven't been able to find me. When they do, they won't show much sympathy. They'll point their guns at me and won't even bother to search for the proper identification: driver's license, fingerprints, work papers would all, in my case, be unwarranted.

My great-grandfather landed in Cuba still dressed in his old frock coat, tuxedo pants, and opera hat and snorting "God, it's hot," as if in Panama it had been cooler than in Havana. In spite of his fallen-wizard's mien, having crossed the Atlantic by Ferdinand de Lessep's side gave him an aura of prestige. They had been good friends, had shared the same dreams: to open a channel of communication between the Old World and the New; to be able to sail from France to India without ever changing course; to reach at last the Orient's swirls of silk, the forests of cinnamon and cayenne, the urns of musk and aloe. But if Ferdinand had dreamed of digging a channel in the virgin continent, which would have been the geographic feat of the century, Albert had dreamed of building the most beautiful bridge in the world, a bridge that would open and close its arches like alligators making love.

Upon the failure of de Lessep's company in 1896, Albert decided not to return to Europe. His vision of a bridge that would bring universal communication to the world had failed, but when he landed in Cuba his curled whiskers were still those of an unpenitent dreamer. As soon as he arrived, he set himself to designing metal bridges, which spread fragile spiderwebs over the tops of mango and bamboo thickets. His bridges offered the islanders a refreshing change from the heavy turdlike pontoons built by the Spaniards on unimaginative dirt roads. His fame spread so that he soon got to be known throughout the island as "the Frenchman of the flying bridges," but Albert never thought much of it, as building bridges was simply his way of making his dreams come true.

Around that time he met the girl he eventually married. Ileana couldn't speak French, and Albert could barely manage to make himself understood in Spanish, but she had been deeply impressed by his whimsical gaze and by the tenderness with which he strung strange webs of threads between his fingers when he attempted to illustrate for her benefit his method for designing bridges.

She would cook potage St. Germain for him and brush his top hat every morning, before kissing him good-bye on the running board of his blue-fringed surrey. While Albert was studying the topographic contours of the island's rivers and waterways, Ileana would spend the day with her aunts and cousins. Together they would oil rifles and guns, count bullets, and prepare bandage rolls and gauze pads, which they would hide under the lid of the family's grand piano. Albert had married into a family of Cuban rebel-patriots, but because he lived in his own world of dreams, he never found out about it.

One day Albert was told that the French lawyer in Paris to whom he had been sending his savings for years had disappeared mysteriously, taking everything with him, and he began to feel crestfallen. The political unrest of the island was making it more and more difficult for him to build his bridges, and he soon found himself out of work. The heat now mortified him more than ever, and he began to dream obsessively of the snow-covered landscapes of his childhood, which he would never see again. It was then he put together the first icebox ever to be built in Cuba, after melting the steel gridirons of one of his unbuilt bridges. He used to sit in it for hours on end, dreaming of the icy bridges and elegant steeples of Paris, as his parched skin at last found relief from the heat.

One morning Ileana couldn't find Albert anywhere. She looked all over the house, coffee cup in hand, calling for him to come for breakfast. She found him sitting frozen inside his icebox, dressed in his old frock coat, tuxedo pants, and frayed silk opera hat, his eyes wide open on the same ghostly landscape, spanned by bridges of all sizes and types, which he had described to her on the day they met.

Ileana took her only son, my grandfather, to live in Matanzas with my rebel great-great-grandmother. The Cuban Revolution was burgeoning: Cacarajícara, Lomas del Tabí, Ceja del Negro; each new uprising threatened to set the island's landscape on fire. Jacobito must have been around seven years old when a traitor's bullet downed *el titán de bronce* in the battle of Punta Brava. Maceo was an old friend of the family's: "He stood up on his stirrups, dropped his machete, and came tumbling down from his horse. There you see the Ceiba tree, those are your cousins, colonels of the army, there he lies dead in your cousin's arms, after they picked him up from where he had fallen, behind enemy lines." Ileana would point out these images to her son again and again, leafing through an old, thumb-worn volume of Cuban history. "They were true revolutionaries, your cousins were. They defied volley after volley to recover the body and later galloped for three nights and three days to bury the body as far as possible from the enemy's vengeful arm."

Jacobito was never impressed by the family's heroic deeds. He was more interested in the colorful fairs and marketplaces of Matanzas, where he would gaze for hours on the spinning wheels of the snow-cone vendors, on the grinding wheels of the knife and scissors sharpeners, on the horse-betting wheels, and on the huge, multicolored blinking Ferris wheel, on which he could never ride because he was too poor. He was, in short, so obsessed by everything that had to do with wheels, that when he turned fifteen his mother sent him to a small town off the southern coast of Puerto Rico aboard a banana sloop, where a distant uncle had a foundry where the catherine wheels of nearby sugar plantations were cast. Puerto Rico was a much poorer island than Cuba, but peace had suddenly made her relatively rich, as business there was going on as usual. There Jacobito would not only be safe from the haphazard surroundings of Matanza's fairs, but he would also be out of reach of the fierce reprisals of the Spaniards, who had by then wiped out most of the family.

Jacobito went ashore at Playa de Ponce, machete in hand, pants rolled up to his knees, straw hat pulled down over his eyebrows, and without a shirt to his name. "I became a machinist's apprentice at El Phoenix, Uncle Theo's foundry, and I immediately took to the idea of an immortal bird which rises again from its ashes. I learned fast; I was soon casting the dizzying catherine wheels of the sugar mills myself and helping my uncle make a profit by them. I loved the work at El Phoenix, because the wheels of the sugar mills reminded me of the spinning wheels of the snow-cone vendors of my faraway hometown. The catherine wheels whizzed, the flywheels whisked, the steam cylinders whistled as they pulled on the axle that pushed on the flywheel that squeezed out the sugar syrup, and before I knew it the Marines had landed in Guánica."

Gallantly done up in his braided fireman's uniform, Jacobito rode Yumuri chest deep into the Caribbean, in order to greet Commander Davis properly. The *Dixie,* the *Annapolis,* and the *Wasp* formed a string of leaden silhouettes against the sleepy seascape of La Playa. The Spanish troops withdrew from the village without firing a single shot, and the key to the city was handed over to Commander Davis in a musical kermess, held to the tune of the firemen's fine brass band.

The next day, when the rest of the troops were about to land, Jacobito drew near to the commander and, with the help of an interpreter, tried to warn him not to set up tent near the Portugués's dry riverbed, as this was a treacherous river given to sudden violent floods. "Our town is a peaceful town," he told him, "you have nothing to fear. Set your tents up in the city square, so that we may get to know you better, and you may mingle freely with us." But the strangeness of the place, the blinding heat, the toads plastered like cardboard cutouts on the dusty streets, the eccentric firehouse with its quizzical red-and-white stripes half-melting under the sun, the cathedral's silver-titted belfries, the Masonic Lodge with its huge eye staring at them from under its whitewashed steeple, were all too intimidating for the young volunteers from Pennsylvania and Illinois, and the Marine columns were ordered to head toward the riverbed.

Commander Davis thanked Jacobito for his well-meant advice. "How did you come into such a splendid specimen of the Tennessee Walker?" he asked Jacobito politely. Jacobito didn't understand what he meant, until the interpreter pointed to Yumurí. "He's not from Tennessee, no, sir; this horse is Puerto Rican by birth, a *paso fino* of the finest breed. He's the son of Batallita in Mejorana, a direct descendant of our country's champion Dulcesueño, but if you like him he's yours, sir, please accept him as my gift, so you'll know what a real horse is like."

The commander didn't understand the business about the lineage very well, but he gladly accepted Jacobito's unexpected gift. "His name is Yumurí. I named him after a famous Indian chief who beat off the invaders in my country. No, sir, of course it wasn't here, it took place in Cuba, where I was born, and the invaders were the Spaniards, they were a very backward people, sir; it was a long time ago."

"You don't mind if I change his name, do you?" the commander asked, looking a bit staggered.

"No, of course not, name him whatever you want."

"How about Tonto, that's a nice name; it's very popular in New Mexico; they use it a lot in rodeos, corridas, and horse shows."

Horse, rider, and Panama hat all spun around of a piece, a rebel weathervane suddenly whipped by the wind. Jacobito didn't even turn his head to take leave of the commander as he rode away. "Tonto! I'll never let him name you Tonto! I hope the river drowns them, Yumurí, it's what they deserve."

In spite of such an inauspicious beginning, the fact was that Jacobito's dreams all came true thanks to the Marines' arrival. He was at once commissioned to build modern metal bridges that would span the bamboo thickets at every difficult bend of the island's rivers, to melt huge quantities of bluishreddishwhitehot steel, which were then poured into the immense molds of the catherine wheels that were needed by the great sugar mills, which were mushrooming up on the island at the time, built by foreign investors. Thus, Jacobito's house was the first in town to be lit up with General Electric lightbulbs, to have a Frigidaire icebox with the condensing coils on top, a Hotpoint electric stove, a sexy black tile bathroom with black American Standard toilet and shower tub, an Electrolux vacuum cleaner, and a Sunbeam electric fan that was so noisy it made you feel you were sitting under the nose of a Pan Am DC-3. He loved to ride through the dusty streets in the town's first Model-T, scaring horses and people alike. One day his admiration for the foreigners reached such a pitch that, after witnessing the daring acrobatics of an American parachute fiend who jumped from his open cockpit to the canefields below, he climbed up on the high gabled roof of his house and hurled himself courageously into space, clasping an open umbrella in his hand.

The whole town followed his wake to the cemetery. His friends, the members of the firemen's band, walked slowly behind his casket, blaring their horns without let-up, their tears mingling with their brass lit-up smiles as they sang:

> *Happy days of love*
> *will never come again*
> *let life be savoured now*
> *by happy and sad alike.*

He wouldn't have liked a solemn funeral; he had never trusted solemn people. And so they buried him in his fireman's uniform, his plumed helmet under his arm and his patent-leather boots shined like new pennies. In compliance with his last wishes as a Freemason, there was no cross at his grave. Grendel, his dog, was laid out upon it, ears alert and fluffy tail raised in farewell forever, as he had been preserved long ago by Jacobito himself, enshrined in a bath of cement.

As a child I used to think about all these things, whenever I sat enthralled, listening to my grandfather's stories. He always told his stories in front of a curious glass box he had had made in Cuba to counter the nostalgia of exile. The hills of coarse green grass made of dyed hay, the little thatched roof huts, the latticework balconies, the cotton-swab clouds stuck to the painted blue sky of the barrio in Matanzas where Jacobito had been born would then all come to life. Farmers with burlap bags over their shoulders would suddenly start walking down winding paths, would start tending their vegetable plots or milking their cows, proud that the land they cared for belonged only to them.

I always suspected the box held an unanswered secret. After my grandfather was gone I would stare at it for a long time, standing unsteadily on tiptoe on one of the wicker chairs in the parlor (the box was always on a high shelf, out of reach of the children). Discouraged because I couldn't decipher what the box was trying to tell me, I'd go out of the house angrily, slamming the door behind me and refusing to play with my cousins, who milled around yelling and running in the yard. I didn't know why I felt so angry, and soon I'd forget all about it.

After my grandfather's death, my grandmother took over the family affairs. My father, Juan Jacobo, was the youngest of her six sons and also the most gifted. Once he took the strings out of the family's grand piano and put them back in such a way that it ended up having a Japanese five-tone scale. My grandmother began to worry when she saw her husband's extravagances begin to crop up in her son. Jacobito, for example, had a passion for lavender African lilies, but he couldn't settle for planting a row or two of them in his garden. To him, planting lavender lilies meant planting an ocean of lilies, so they would overflow from one island town to the next, and he could build new bridges to cross over them.

His grandfather's old dream of universal communication haunted him, and he went into politics as the only way to carry out Albert's vision of a bridge that would span both the Northern and the Southern hemispheres.

"Last night I dreamed I was building the most beautiful bridge in the world," he told me one day, "a bridge of silver strands that stretched from north to south, from east to west, and the strands kept coming out of me as if I were a giant spider and not an engineer. Isn't it strange? My bridge joined the world into a single nation where there was no war or hunger or poverty; thousands of birds came to nest in our forests, and those who sighted us from afar would cry: 'This island is indeed an Afortunada because it has helped us find peace.' "

At that time the island was torn by an ever-more violent struggle between statehood and independence. Politicians squabbled endlessly about status, becoming richer by the minute, while the country became poorer and poorer. Juan Jacobo believed his bridge would be the answer to the country's problems. He advised the people to forget about the age-old feud between statehood and independence and to concentrate on eliminating poverty. He traveled to Washington, where he convinced Congress to help turn the island into a "showcase for the South." The island would be the first place on earth where Latin American faith in the values of the spirit would blend with Anglo-Saxon respect for the law, faith in democracy, and technological progress.

Soon millions of dollars in federal funds began to pour into the island. Playing his tune in every town square like the Pied Piper of Hamelin, Juan Jacobo won the country's poor to his campaign, so that they followed him everywhere. He promised them lampposts, public telephones, air-conditioned buses, Christmas bonuses, municipal orchestras, homes for the aged, even free meals for the orphaned and the poor. Foreigners who visited the island couldn't get over the spectacle of Juan Jacobo, the millionaire, being the champion of the city's poor, idolized in every shantytown from La Perla to Chichamba.

But Juan Jacobo's dream of turning the island into a universal bridge was doomed to failure. Latin American countries, envious of the island's progress, thought it was being used by the United States for covert purposes; they looked down on the islanders for having sold out to North American interests. In the United States, the islanders were still considered Latin Americans and were never seen as completely trustworthy. The professional island politicians, on the other hand, did all they could to fuel the status controversy. It did them no good to have a united country working together to banish poverty; the controversy between statehood and independence was for them a lucrative affair. In view of the growing mistrust in his dream of a universal bridge, Juan Jacobo began to feel dispirited. A bridge, he thought then, was, after all, something to be trod upon by those who knew where they were coming from, or at least where they were going. But the people of the island had no idea of either, and therefore it was better if it was never built.

Juan Jacobo renounced his dream and devoted himself to strengthening the family fortune. With the help of foreign capital he built more and more factories and became richer by the day. Of all the family members, he was the only one to keep a heart unspoiled. Like King Midas, everything he touched turned to gold. He even went so far as to feel a certain nostalgia for poverty, but he needn't have worried because gold went through his hands like a sieve. His fingers were hardened with gold dust, but the clothes he wore were always somewhat threadbare; his cuffs frayed, and the hems of his pants trailed baggily after him. The scent of fresh lemons that filled the room every time he took out his handkerchief to mop his brow, the gesture of his hand poised fleetingly in the air when he began to speak—everything about him suggested the genteel politeness of a cavalier gentleman of a bygone age. Before he was forty he had lost everything he owned, trying to help out his friends in need.

On the day he met Marina, an ocean of lilies stirred up waves of passion in his eyes. He married her after a short courtship, during which she let him know she would be both master and mistress of the house. She was the one to spruce up the family each year at Easter time. On Easter Sunday she would decorate the hallways with ferns and poinsettias, have the servants polish the floor and the furniture, and then tell us children to get the good china and silverware from the cupboard. We would then set the table for twelve and go out to the slums in search of our dinner guests. When we came back, the dwellers of the glass box would have suddenly come to life. I can almost see them as they stretch their limbs to move about dispiritedly, dragging their bare feet across the tile floor Mother made me scrub so hard this morning. They leave their burlap sacks on the floor along with their bunches of bananas and plantains, and gingerly begin to sit at the table, as if they didn't know how to move, how to lean on the carved chairs without splintering the mahogany roses, how to place their weatherbeaten hands on the snow-white tablecloth. My mother blesses the food from the head of the table. My aunts and uncles begin to pass the porcelain platters among the guests, the steak and onions, the rice and beans, with painstaking care, so as not to let a single grain of rice, a single drop of sauce, stain the immaculate white tablecloth. Little by little heads begin to look up from sunken chests, glances are exchanged with more confidence, a toothless mouth timidly rehearses a grin, and the dwellers of the glass box seem happy once again.

Every Christmas, on Three King's Day, my mother's Easter ritual would be observed in reverse. We would then be sent by our parents to the slums to be the guests of our guests. On those occasions we loved to pretend that we were entering grandfather's glass box, as we jumped from plank bridge to plank bridge, puddle to puddle, balcony to balcony, frightening the pigs, the chickens, the guinea hens, the billy goats, just for the pleasure of hearing them bleat until the moment came to pass out our gifts solemnly among the children, wrapped, as always, in glistening silver foil with huge poinsettias tied on with red bows.

The gift-giving ceremony would last all morning, but by noon we'd be sitting patiently in a rusty zinc shed. The shed was punched full of holes, and the sun lit restless fireflies over our heads as the aunts, uncles, and parents of our young friends began to spread out a splendid banquet before us. Platters heaped with baby goat stew, steaming cauldrons of rice and chicken, suckling pig served on plantain leaves and decorated with fire-red hibiscus, *mazamorra, majarete,* and *mundo nuevo,* the stream of dishes was endless. We'd never be able to eat it all; we were already stuffed to the gills. "We've had enough already, thank you, it was delicious." "You can't mean it, dear, you haven't tried anything yet. Taste this last bit of *longaniza,* this littlest bit of *butifarra,* we made it especially for you."

We knew we had to sit there and eat it all up; there simply was no getting around it until all the platters were empty and the mongrel dogs under the table would begin to lick our bare legs clean. Only then would the slum children stop watching us without blinking; only then would we be able to get up and play hopscotch, marble-in-the-hole, and hide-and-seek with them, to the tune of the guinea hen's *"yapaqué, yapaqué";* only then would we be allowed into the latrine, where it was such fun to go standing up, cooling your behind thanks to the breeze that seeped through the chinks in the wall; only then could we fly the kite, skip the rope, spin the top, tralala, fiddle dee dee, come and make merry together, you and me.

Many years later I came back to the island, having finally acquired my engineering degree. Mother and Father had been dead for some time, having died tragically in an airplane accident. The witnesses to those Biblical banquets—uncles, aunts, and cousins—had expanded the family business to new heights. I had no money of my own, but I asked them to give me a job and until now I have led a peaceful life. I dress carefully every morning, blue serge suit, white shirt, striped tie, and head for my uncle's office. By now I am well versed in the rhythm of production and depreciation of factories; I am what you might call completely assimilated into the environment. Today, however, I've made up my mind finally to find out the secret of the box. I'll slip into my grandparents' old home during the family auction; I'm sure no one will pay attention to me. My relatives, faced with the crisis the family business has recently been going through, are too desperate to notice. Several days ago they agreed, because of impending bankruptcy, to auction off the house and the family heirlooms, which they had till then so reverently preserved.

I step silently across the hall and walk rapidly toward the dining room. To my right, the haggling and wrangling goes on, all family loyalties severed where profit is at stake. "How much do you want to pay for the silver candelabra? Ten, fifteen, sixteen hundred? Will anyone pay two hundred? They're worth a lot more than they were appraised for, after all; we're not going to take advantage of each other, are we? Grandfather's clock, how much do you want to pay for grandfather's clock? It still chimes and grandfather's been silent dust now for some time. Going, going, gone for two hundred and fifty, that's a good buy, let me tell you, much better than the moth-eaten piano nobody wants."

I place my hands over my ears and walk into the darkness of the living room. The uproar of the auction still hasn't reached this part of the house; the old wicker armchairs with carved headrests are still in place, as if waiting for ghosts to sit on them; the glass box is still on its high shelf, covered by a fine layer of dust. I lift it up tenderly with an ease that surprises me; I always thought it was heavy and it's so light. I tuck it under my arm and walk out into the street with it.

I feel I must hurry; I haven't much time left. My bridge will be the last one ever to be built by my family: it will be at once beautiful and frightening. I mingle with the crowds for a few minutes, until the bus to Playa Ponce goes by. I let out a sigh of relief as I sit next to a lottery vendor and listen to him advertise today's lucky number, an islander's "one-way ticket to Paradise." Once I reach the wharf, I get off the bus and quickly locate the schooner in which I am to sail. I look toward the elegant suburb where our family house still stands. Because I'm relatively safe now, I can wait patiently until the detonator hidden on the same shelf where the glass box used to sit finally goes off. I feel happy at last. I know I'll find peace, once the burning arches of my bridge spread out toward the north and toward the south.

MARJORIE AGOSÍN

Translated by Elizabeth Horan

Adelina

E MMA WEISS had never seen the sea, although
she imagined that it was copper-colored like the un-
tamable hair of her Viennese ancestors and of her mother,
Frida Weiss, who wore it bundled up, tied in a blue loop
as if the knotted secrets of her wanderings and rivals were
guarded within. The sea always looked like an unfath-
omable horizon, or like her dreams, like music from the
bottom of the water that Emma Weiss invented every
evening in the remote landscapes of Osorno, Chile, where
the silence and the obscurity of the meadows swarmed,
and the whistling of the animals predicted change and the
births of children and trees.

Her father had escaped long before the tattoos of war.
They say that he had done so through an act of love and
faith. In love with an exquisite and brave cabaret singer
who worked in the all-night districts of the city, he had
decided, once and for all, to declare an end to this illicit
love. In the month of June, when it was possible to walk
about in free air and the incomprehensible smell of wild-
flowers filled the fullness of the air, Joseph Weiss decided
to sprout from the last corner of Vienna and go to Val-

paraíso, city of ports and sun-lit hills. Thus, he bid good-bye, fearful, to Adelina, to her swift legs and spangled suit, because he foresaw, through her maddening habits, her insinuating and defeated wrinkles, the beginnings of the crash, the senseless bombardments, and the indisputable failure of all menace and war. They said goodbye in the plaza with the certainty of those who remain loving one another, near to the earth and to the curve of kisses. They even chose the festivity of the place, where entire families were frolicking, as if they were immortal, because sunshine and children played on the old wooden benches.

Emma Weiss prepared herself for the trip to Valparaíso, and for the first time she would come close to smelling the sea, to seeing its swell and its mystery for all its splendor and delirium. Emma Weiss would also meet her grandmother, Elena, who had remained closed up in the cellar of the house of Adelina, because she was the mother of José Weiss, because she was Jewish. One had to watch out in the city, to circle around the streets before heading for the cellar, to take note very early in the morning that no one was observing. Adelina was liable to enter on the sly, offering peace and her smile delivered as a sustenance into Elena's slender hands. Together, the two women remembered José Weiss and they closed the shutters to light a candle, to illuminate the dead souls and to remember that Jewish navigator who arrived like a soul in trial, descending from the deepest part of his strangled destiny to the strange skirts of Valparaíso with a child of a few months in his arms.

The night before the trip on the train from Osorno to Valparaíso, Emma Weiss ironed her violet linen dress, she brushed her thick, sober hair over and over and again she dreamed of her grandmother Elena and of the sea. She desired it with the innocence of first things, as when she looked at herself naked under the shutters of her room and became beautiful in a dawning roundness. She imagined herself bathed in the sea, letting the water fill her with life and people her with seaweed, and she slept as if the sea had entered her eyes, as if the stories of terror, of the children sent away on the trains of dementia, had been buried in the very cortex of the gulfweed.

In the train they travelled through enormous pastures, past humble, defeated animals, and the smell of smoke impregnating the landscape no longer reminded them of a Europe split in two, for they were rescued in time, thanks to the love of Adelina, who permitted José Weiss to arrive on the Chilean coast before he received a detention order.

Emma Weiss' hands were sweating. It seemed a day of false summer. She rarely glanced at her father who still wore his hat from Vienna and the look of Adelina in his deep green eyes.

The port seemed disorderly, as if God or the constant earthquakes had deliberately forgotten to assemble Valparaíso and the port, and the city seemed rather like a cord of unruly, combed hair and the hills were the size of the people. Maybe that's why it didn't seem strange when Emma Weiss saw a coffin coming down a hill or a bride running over the stony ground.

The day was an intense blue and the sky mingled with the sea. Emma Weiss had already spied the ship on which her grandmother, Elena, whom she had never seen, would arrive. Meanwhile Elena, in the ship, could not stop remembering when she herself, with the intuition of a clairvoyant, had urged Joseph to leave. Kissing him on the hair in silence, she had offered a blessing for the traveller. But José Weiss was thinking of Adelina in the shiny blouse that she would put on in the fatal nights, before the specters of death and of bombs that seemed like black doves swathed in feathers of bad luck.

The hands of Emma Weiss were sweating; she loosened the violet bow and her hair more and more resembled copper-colored algae. Someone tossed paper streamers, and she timidly threw a few of them into the sea, thinking they might fall in her grandmother's hair. And there was the pious sea, receiving the emigrants, pressing on their boat and the padlocks of their souls, while Emma already belonged to the sea, for she had dreamed that her body was a cradle of fish in its lap. Then, suddenly, José saw Elena Weiss. There she was coming with her same tulle hat, smaller, thin-faced, her hair carrying the memory of many deaths. But she understood that she had chosen to live, and she saw Joseph with his summer smile too and his eyes like the forests.

The anxious families tossed paper streamers. Others played little crinkled paper horns that resonated with the splendor of the sloping hills and someone saw from afar a bride dancing along the summits. Valparaíso was strange, perched as if on wings and crazy in its sanity while the sailors streamed out from the ship along with people who were bidding love goodbye and people whose bodies had been battered by the furies of war.

Then, Elena Weiss, dignified, stepped down from the cabin and made out the eyes of her son; she made out her granddaughter, Emma, who looked at her with all the delirium and illusion of her thirteen years. She calmly kissed them because she knew she had arrived at a safe haven and she asked for a drink of water, and she handed Joseph a little folded envelope.

Emma Weiss was happy that she had a grandmother who could embrace and see her father and who gave her a present, a golden blouse that had a strange mixture of splendor and poverty, like her family's bonds.

ANGELA DE HOYOS

Xochitl-Poem: For Paul Perry, Joseph Booker, and the Palo Alto Writers Guild

I

... for that day when we shall
all sit down, being noble
ladies and gentlemen of leisure
—and I say leisure, because Time
is a pristine luxury few of us
in the 20th Century can afford—
to share the eloquence of
the simple word, the transcendental
thought, the visceral feeling

when, submerging inhibitions
in the creative waters,

our molecules will
touch and repel, touch
and repel

at times hesitating
to drag out from ancestral closets
our preconceived notions
transparent as the nakedness
of rain

because the poetic process
is such a very
very personal, a very
private thing

. . . meanwhile the dormant
nahualli within us
grows rabid, we bite
our tongues raw to swallow
the red hot coal
of pain
—to check the carcinoma
before it can
spread, before it can
devour others

I I

and the whys the wherefores
freeze, unanswered
in the death's-head

eyes of Wednesday's child, scrawny
hands clawing the air to
reach us, teeth chattering
begging us to intercede . . .
useless to explain
that we have been
up to the mountain and
the word is *nada,* we have
accomplished nothing;
to the contrary, we the poets
now stand accused: like Vivaldi
we keep repeating
over and over
the same theme . . .

III

then someone taps us gently
on the shoulder, wakes us
into sleep. And the miracle
of birth—this *xochitl* poem, this
innocent gift of love—
redeems us.

In Aztek Nahuatl, *nahualli,* or *nahual,* refers to the animal spirit within us; *xochitl* means "flower."

MIREYA ROBLES
Translated by Angela de Hoyos

In the Other Half of Time

THE WOMAN with Carthaginian eyes was looking towards the sea, and her gaze extended through many centuries. It was a ritual. It was a rite. A rite. To meet with the past in the silent vastness, in the vague murmur of briny foam. The morning, fresh, and the silence profiling her contours. She knew that she had lived many reincarnations and the past, without file cards in its fingers, did away with data. But there she was, the weight of millenary tensions, and the sea. And above all, that sensation of destiny: a certain place and a date. Like a tryst, concerted prior to birth. It was just a matter of meeting. It was a matter of converting the daily death into expectancy. It was a matter of visualizing the silhouette of that other being, at the other end of the tenseness of time, plowing through breath and space, or immobile, overcoming the wounds of a stagnant yearning, retracing the veins of the skin to rest in the warmth of the hands. The meeting. It was a matter of meeting. And beyond, on the shore, the moist sand seemed to contain all the atoms of the echo. Resonance, voice: reply. The woman, untouched by common hands that roll pennies and coins, let herself be caressed by the air, by a breeze that penetrated her deep silence. Behind had remained the house that once in other centuries had been inhabited by slaves. Rites to the African deities. Possessions of spirits that spoke through the voice of the medium. Intermittent messages from other epochs that persisted in flowing together with the present. But the north-star voice that should indicate the meeting place never materialized nor was ever heard amid the messages hurled by those who fell into a trance.

Once again facing the sea, open to the suggestions of those echoes that contained her past. The waves, like docile workers, deposited in the slowness of their gestures pieces of timber, strips of algae, bottle caps, flasks. A flask. A flask of perfume. The woman's hand gathered the flask and hugging it with her soft firmness, brought it to her closest silence. Her glance fell upon the strange facets, the atomizer, on that fluid, wounded by the sun's rays, that had the consistency of oils and ointments. She let the aroma touch her flesh, and she felt, as in other ages, already prepared to quit a precinct, this time, an open precinct, towards the search. With a movement out of long habit, she placed the perfume upon the skin of sand that served as her dressing table. And she directed her glance towards the timber. Towards that piece of timber that lay there, patiently, as if it were waiting for her. She felt between her hands the dampness of the thick fragment of log, and she tried to decipher the strange letters that formed a message in a language that was now unknown to her. She noticed that the plaque was meticulously halved in two, and she drew to her bosom the humid letters, as if embracing them. Without knowing exactly what was happening, she thought she understood. She raised herself slowly, and with a firm step she went overtaking the remoteness of the beach. In the distance, the station. And in the isolation of the rails, the lonely trains. A ticket. The conductor with his visor cap. The rapid movement of successive images. And over the loudspeakers, a name, a town. And over the loudspeakers, a name, a town.

She waited for the train's definitive stop. She felt herself go down the ramp, and suddenly, she was on the railway platform. The expanding group of passengers went scattering, space inside, taking their luggage, greetings, embraces. In the vacated space of the platform, the silhouette of a woman. Her glance intense, her contour engraved in the silence. Immobile, and in her hands, the half of a length of timber, and strange letters.

A brief pause. Yearned-for peace. The breath gasping and deep. They advanced so as to shorten the distance. They looked into each other's eyes, and they recognized one another.

CECILE PINEDA

from Face

IN THE SKY a cloud is forming. The head, the shoulders appear. It is May. There is a leaden grey outline lifting the white of the clouds in relief. The blue of the sky is cold, wintry. There is a greenish cast to the light. The sun is absent.

A wind forms across the bay. The expanse of water marks its restlessness in the apparently static crests and troughs. From this distance, the waves appear not to move—curls arrested on a tightly coifed head. They do not move at all. Looking, then looking away, then rapidly looking again, one can only seem to catch a movement, more imperceptible than breath itself. Or perhaps the waves are the same, the same crests as before. Or perhaps they have only moved one trough closer to the shore, shifting slightly, as if in a viewfinder.

In the sky, the cloud has changed now. The head is lowered, or perhaps it has turned around, or the shoulders have risen to ward off a blow. No more. The giant is gone. Other shapes are forming.

One stair, at the top, is etched with a crack now. The concrete in the vein has crumbled. Little pebbles, aggregates of dust perhaps, have settled in the interstices. A child worrying the cracks could dislodge them with a grubby finger. A child gazing out to sea (past the hook of land), letting his vacant eyes roam the shapes of giants left by the wind, by the clouds as they move, vacant eyes puzzling the stillness of waves that move only when the gaze is averted.

The man stands there, not thinking of anything, fighting the stiff wind with each intake of air—the breath fought for, briefly denied, then won. Each time. Even with this wind, even at this height, the waves seem to hold their very breath. Still moving, they barely move at all. This is the sky he can see every morning. This is the bay which on calm days seems barely to breathe from this height.

The man stands to the left, a little behind the child, watching him idly. The child squats on the landing, worrying the crack. Perhaps some small dirt clod is wedged between his nail and finger cap. He studies it for a moment. The moment stretches, then snaps as, once again, he bends to his examination. An insect, perhaps an ant, traces its path in the vein, now emerging from the crack, now disappearing. The man stands watching. A handkerchief covers his face; it is white, cotton (not linen). The corner, which hangs below his chin, flutters in the wind. The man stands there as if his hands are in his pockets. He does not move. This is the only pavement, this and the steps which stretch down the cliff face, switching back below, disappearing from sight long before reaching the water.

The man can see far down, to the point where the stairs are lost to view behind a jutting outcrop. Even the thin strands of grass there have difficulty holding their purchase. There are no trees, only the slate rock, the dead grasses assaulted by the wind. The surf is hidden altogether by the rock.

People have always lived here, before remembering, building their shacks high above the city from its discards: cardboard, corrugated tin, sheets of green plastic, potato and rice sacks, tar paper. Even the earth is greasy from its steady human traffic. Rain, when it falls, forms globules before dissolving beneath the dusty surface of water left to gather in the oil drums. Along the gutters, open sewers run.

It is grey now. The wind brings with it the chill of June, the smell of wood burning, the snap of wet bedclothes strung like sails against the wind. The boy stirs. Out of the corner of his eye, his glance has caught the open shoes, the dusty feet. He turns quickly to see the man standing there, hands in his pockets, face hidden behind the white handkerchief.

The man watches as the boy, still running, appears on the ledge below, smaller, still running, disappearing, now reappearing on a terrace far below, smaller still, still running, again disappearing.

"Mamae, Mamae." His cry is lost far below.

A solitary bird spreads its wings to the wind. The man shades his eyes against the glare.

THERE IS barely time, barely time before the post office closes. He pushes the transmittal slip deep into his pocket. He begins to run. The bay reflects the play of lightning across its face. He can feel the first drops, icy, against his face and arms, and the smell, curious, acrid, the kind of sulphurous toying in the nostrils of rain long overdue. He is running—past the washlines stripped only moments ago by women even now making for the dry of their shacks.

He is running now, seeing without seeing the stairs, stained now with the first drops of rain. He is running, running down stairs only moments ago filled with people sprinting to bring their wash in from the downpour. He runs, now down one flight, now down another. He sees without seeing the wet of the slope, the fury of wind-lashed clouds stampeding the sky. He sees without seeing the small boy squatting on the landing, with his stick tracing a crack in the rock. Water soaks his shoes. A cold membrane of slime sends his soles skating over the leather.

He is heading for the post office, the transmittal slip crumpled and probably already wet in his pocket. He remembers this instant in which his running gives way, the instant of running when the stairs take on a running of their own. He remembers that moment when the ground fails before sending him arcing over the abyss.

Mother!

Had it come from him? Was it his own black cry?

Mother of God!

It seemed to him then it was his mother's voice.

He can hear her scream above the roaring of the waters. He is plummeting, spinning, caught in a gigantic saucer, spinning sky, water, its black mouth yawning upward.

Mother!

His body catapults over the water, whipped by a gale. The stairs curl upward, surging like waves, smashing up through him, splintering—shards of light inside his head.

The small boy sends his stick spinning over the edge.

Mamae! Mamae! He is running toward the row of shacks fronting the steps.

Mamae!

A door opens. A hand reaches out to pull him clear of the storm into the comforting darkness.

"Someone fell down there. A man. Down there by the rocks."

He pulls her hand. They stumble together through the downpour. They come to where the man lies crumpled. They stand shivering, uncertain. Already her thin dress is soaked and clinging.

"Is he dead?"

She leans closer, studying him. The boy stares in the dreamy way of children. From under the man's head, blood seeps. He follows the sharp red tendrils as they blur into rain.

THROUGH THE PILLOW he can hear muffled sounds.

"Good morning." A man's voice, a doctor perhaps. He moves his index, his entire hand to acknowledge the voice.

"We'll take a look at you today."

Today. How long has he been like this, here in this sack? He has lost count. Only throbbing marks the passing of days he remembers better as absence. *Today.* He feels a pang of what? Dread? Regret, perhaps?

Scissors gnaw at the darkness. He can hear them distinctly, and the rasp of adhesive tearing. He can feel the gauze unwinding. No pain, or very little as the layers fall open like swaddling. He remembers the light stabbing at his eyes.

He sees the man in his white jacket through an aura at first, and the two women, and as he grows accustomed to the light, their starched headcaps. One grasps a clipboard.

It was a telegram. He remembers now. His mother was dying.

One woman removes the tray with its soiled bandages and snarls of adhesive. The other soaks a gauze sponge. He can see her distinctly. She dabs at his skin with alcohol. There is no smell. At first he only vaguely wonders at it. No smell at all.

He can see something in their eyes. What, he is not sure. He remembers thinking *is it so bad as that?*

LATELY, HE HAS BEEN THINKING. He sits overlooking the harbor, before first light, before even the slum alley roosters greet the day in their dusty ghetto splendor. He is recalling the advance and retreat of the nurses, the doctors the surgeons, the medical students.

and here we have the knee, the arm, the eardrum . . .

Always scaling new heights. And the loudspeaker imploring, directing, choreographing the skirmishes, the engagements.

And here we have the face . . .

They have arranged the dressing to yield on cue, like an important unveiling. "And here, Gentlemen, after almost two months . . ." (he holds his breath) ". . . and here after almost two months . . ." The bandage lifts, the sunlight of morning stabs his eyes.

To him, their intake of breath is like a roar. When has he heard this sound? at his birth? at his death?

I saw the angel in the heavens and the sound of the great trumpet came to me.

When?

"We have the face of Senhor Helio Cara!"

Who is he? Who has he become, with his name of a stranger?

"Yes, Cara. The irony is not lost on you, I see."

But already he has held his breath too long. He feels the hot tears. And hears the voice:

"Never has this service seen such an injury. Mr. Cara . . ." and the swallowed giggles of the medical students, standing at white-starched attention, suppressing the whispering of their linen, ". . . such an injury."

THE SHACKS of the Whale Back have always appeared open somehow, row on row, along alleys that run straight or nearly straight. He never noticed, until now, how honeycombed they are, clustering like the nests of swallows—or wasps—clutching tightly at the hillside.

He should have been prepared. Nearly three months it had been. The tramway leaves him with only a short distance of walking uphill. At that hour (it's something after noon) and even in this season, the heat pounds overhead, his face throbs behind the mask. The dirt path is steep, steeper than he remembers.

And the shacks! He never realized—before—how stacked they are against the slope, tumbling, scrambling like clumsy, eyeless dwarves, their window openings dark against the fierce light of the noonday sun. Why had he never noticed how rutted the ground was, and powdery the earth except in those dank places the sun never reaches where rivulets of ghostly moisture cause moss to cushion the black slime of the gutters, so dark that even at noon a speck of crumpled foil winks deceivingly—like an eyeless sardine decaying in the wet.

He should have been prepared. But trudging up the slope in his open shoes, through the faintness and the ache, his thoughts shut off, he struggles to place one foot before the other, intent only on this last stretch, ignoring the torment of sweat, unable to mop it, trapped as it is behind the mask. He has reached his threshold at last.

For a moment he imagines the door gapes open in welcome. But what is the scatter of strange things over the ground—pieces of crumpled newspaper, a dented metal cup, a shaving brush? He stands in the doorway taking stock. His shadow travels across the room and comes to rest where the cupboard lies, knocked over and broken. And in the corner where his cot had stood, only the empty metal frame is left, its springs warped and sagging, the mattress, the blanket—gone.

Quickly he skirts the pile of refuse on the ground. In the shed, through the opening in the wall opposite, he rips up the rotted floorboard. The box is there, its red and blue scrolls faded now. It is still there. He reaches below to pull it out. He slides the drawer open. Still there. Before he counts the coins, he glances over his shoulder. No one there to see. He spills the contents on the floor. They are his last cruzeiros. He counts them. He will have to work at once if he is to hold on to the little he has saved.

He feels tired all of a sudden. He lets the coins filter through his fingers and slide back into the box. He slips the cover in place before lowering it once more under the floorboards. They had not found it. It was safe.

HE HAS BECOME a creature of the night. He has learned to feel his way along the familiar ruts behind the Whale Back. The mercury arc lights of the embarcadero give him his bearings. He heads for the dark, bottle-strewn alleys, the mews behind the big tourist restaurants and hotels. He wears the brown fedora, discolored now, the ribbon stained with sweat. Over his face he wears the handkerchief, tied at the back, the knot held in place by the crown.

It is the limbo hour when the last drunken tourists lurch back to their luxury hotels overlooking the bay, drunk on batidas, their steamy heads filled with the scent of negresses, their bodies glistening with promise. It is the hour before the first sweepers and vegetable carts make their way clattering along the paving stones of the back alleys, before the city begins to stir in its sleep.

He has learned to scout the best locations, to find the garbage bins brimming with the evening's most opulent discards: vegetables, fruits still waiting to be peeled, and the ungnawed bones of a clientele too well-bred or bored to have picked them clean. Sometimes, if he is lucky, he finds a steak intact, before the packs of stray dogs roaming the streets at night can get to it.

He rounds the corner. The green glow of a mercury lamp spills his shadow far ahead of him into the darkness. Ahead lies a dumpster, its red paint battered by the garbage handlers, filled to overflowing. He sets his basket to rest on the cobblestones of the curb. Bending high over the edge he peers down at the boxes. He lifts them out onto the curb to uncover the night's leavings.

The harvest is a thin one. He finds two mangoes black with age and chayote. It will do for soup. And reaching still lower, he finds an onion already furry with mold. Below these are islands of moist leavings, cold and clammy in the obscurity—farofa perhaps, or some kind of polenta. He is satisfied with the fruits, the vegetables. These he places carefully in the basket. Then one by one he reloads the cartons back in place to cover all traces of his foraging, like the night predators he has come to know, who like himself prowl the same alleys of the same limbo as he. In the city at sleep, in the deserted alleys, or in the Whale Back, he had come to know them, the creatures that roamed at night, parasites that fed, like himself, on the leavings of the day, of those not afraid to show their faces in the back alleys, or even the streets.

He had never imagined this underground when he had been one of them, the small mice and occasional rats he had come to discover, hunting like himself, some alone, or in packs, always on the move, some (like him) covering their traces, others leaving mounds of disorder to mark their passing.

But of the other creatures, those of his own kind, he is less knowing: Indians from the Interior living on the outskirts, roaming like night creatures, restless, always on the move, never even pausing to build a shelter. The mill hands locked out since the strikes, and the fugitives from the police squads, some of them, too, must roam the streets, but in a night different from his. His night is of a separate kind. Either way, with the white handkerchief, or without its protection, he has learned to come and go unseen.

THE DISTRICT close to the terminal is dimly lit. Here and there neon signs proclaim a garage or an all-night hotel. He keeps close to the arcades, now and again ducking under an awning. A few late stragglers make their way through the half-empty streets, too huddled against the wet to take much notice of him.

Even at such a late hour, long lines of travelers wait at the depot, clutching their bundles as they queue up at the ticket counters. He takes his place in line before the window.

He is last in line behind a woman with three small children. The youngest sees him and begins to cry. The woman looks at him briefly. She clutches the boy's head tightly against her thigh, hiding his face in her skirt. Another man (in the line for Oriente) glances, turns away. And then a family hurries past, burdened with boxes and packages tied with twine. They are running to board a departing bus. The woman's voice screams hysterically. "Will you be quiet?" her husband growls. Abruptly, she falls silent as she catches sight of him.

The crowd around him, pressed almost shoulder to shoulder when he first arrived, has thinned. An invisible white silence gathers around him like a zone.

"Round trip, Senhor?" the agent asks.

"One way."

The white zone shadows him in the waiting room. He finds a place on the bench of polished slats. He can feel the movement of heads, first turning just enough to look, then fast away, the waves of passengers, standing first in their private limbos of waiting, their place defined now by how far or near they find themselves to him.

"Mama, look! Why does he have a handkerchief?" asks a tiny boy before a hissing woman yanks his arm.

The white zone has its particular density: whispers, furtive glances, the panicked cries of children, all exile him. Each movement, gesture, sound is known to him. Now that man will hunch a little deeper into himself, now another will blow his nose. Now a woman will take reassurance from it: he has a nose at least, let alone a face. A mother will quiet a balky child with a sweet saved for just such an occasion, and in the slow deliberate way she unwraps it, seek to divert her child's attention. Like the movement of birds pecking for mollusks in the surf, sensing the imminent threat of each encroaching wave, hurrying to stay just clear of it, so the waiting room adjusts to the huge intrusion of his handkerchief, his hat.

At last the loudspeaker announces his departure. He gets up now, lifts the suitcase wearily. If they could (if custom did not prevent it), they would scatter before him like seabirds, like waves.

He finds the platform in the darkened street outside, mounts the ridged metal steps, hands the driver his crumpled ticket. Then, carefully, he threads his way through the narrow aisle to the last seats where he will be of no dismay to anyone—if he is fortunate.

THE BUS CLIMBS the steeply winding road, into the mountains, seven hundred kilometers distant from the capital. On the rare occasions when he could afford the trip home, his mother lay there, not saying anything. He remembers her hair, once jet, toward the end became a tangle of stark white, yanked upward from the temples as though she dreamed of horsemen in the night.

He remembers the last time. The neighbor woman has made her a bed of linen sheets, and she lies there, barely moving, her hands clasped together, empty now of work, warding off the night. She wakes only rarely, her eyelids flutter, her eyes inside their sockets seem not to focus at all, or hardly. Yet, when she opens them, she lifts her arms, thin and transparent as chicken wings, to embrace and cradle him. It is then she begins a kind of song, a rhythmic sighing, more like a moan. She is a long time dying, as if before she could break the habit of her living, she must shake her life free of all its grief, must pour it out in the soft moans of an ancient child.

He sits by the bedside, touching the transparent parchment of her hands, the veins so thin they must adhere together. Yet she breathes. The lungs do their work, perversely running away with the bit of her life still in their teeth. She is barely sixty.

She appears not to hear him speaking to her. He places his mouth against her bones so she can hear him: "Aie, what songs you sing." He thinks he catches the ghost of a smile. But already the bones under the coverlet are curled like a skeleton's hugging its mouthfuls of earth. Will he ever say of her that she is dead? Or does she carry the seeds of her death, even now, in the pinched, white nostrils that struggle for breath?

The road levels out between two ranges of hills, then abruptly shuts tight as it winds still higher, once more to narrow between the muddy unpaved streets, the shacks of corrugated tin and tar paper at the edge of the town, the rush fences, the varicolored washlines of rags that flap in the sun, the mangy dogs, the barefoot children scampering about the grease tins with their choked geraniums struggling against the dust.

CAREFULLY HE PROPS the piece of mirror against the wall. In it he studies what he sees there. Calmly, for the first time, he forces his eyes to take the measure of his mangled face.

Have the traces of her dying come back to shape his dreams: the dusty bottles? the matches? the syringe? Where has it come from, this idea? Has it hovered for some time, like the dust particles suspended in the sickroom air?

He would make himself a face. He did not have to wait. He would make it here, where he knew no one anymore, where no one could tell him how he had to look, what he had to be—now that he had fallen—now he no longer belonged, even to himself. There was no one here to say it, to say it could not be done. Or that he might not do it, that he had no right. No one at all.

UNDER THE WHITE SACKING of the market awnings, the momentary brightness of the sun declares a truce. It softens the faces of the passersby, and the countryfolk who sit patiently on the ground, their blankets spread with beans, with rice or cumin, with a gentle glow. The spring wind ruffles the awnings and makes them flutter in the breeze, gently, flapping them from time to time. And he, it is as if he wears their reflection on his face: a small handkerchief, no longer white, sometimes fluttering—like the awnings—when the wind blows.

Searching in the marketplace, he finds it, at last: the very thin thread, thinner than the ordinary cotton thread he is used to, not quite so thin as the spider gossamer his mother used to stem the bleeding when he cut himself.

"How much?"

The countryman gazes at him through milky eyes. A weathered hand reaches up from under his blanket to grasp the spool. He brings it almost to within an inch of his eyes.

"Five."

"Five?" It seems too cheap.

"Five."

He pulls a ten-cruzeiro coin from his pocket lining and hands it to him. The old man drops it somewhere in the depths of his overalls. His hand emerges at last with the change, which he tenders with the spool.

In the side street under the arcades, a scissor vendor

displays his wares. In the recess, dark even at noon, his assistant, a boy of no more than ten, works the grindstone. Sparks fly. The sound travels on this day of sun and warmth, as if filtered through an accordion. He stands before the stall, fumbling in his pocket. The scissors he brings up are worn, nicked and, here and there, discolored. He gives them to the vendor.

"How much to sharpen?"

The man considers, scratches his stubbly jaw.

"Like this? Ten. Now if they weren't so worried . . ."

"Five," he counters.

"No. No, friend." The vendor hands them back to him. "Listen, my assistant alone costs me ten a day."

Again the vendor looks at the scissors. He considers silently. "Make it eight."

"Eight," he agrees.

Inside the shop, the boy has stopped the wheel, and stands polishing the knife with a cloth. From outside he can see its luster, glinting in the obscurity.

"Jacinto . . . here."

The boy spins the grindstone.

THE ROOM IS READY. He slides the crate which will serve him as a counter against the wall adjacent to the dresser. The water pot is there now, standing half-full on the ring over the butane burner, the box of matches next to it. He takes up the matchbox, slips open the drawer with his left thumb. He removes one match, which he holds between his right thumb and index finger. He snaps the box closed with his left middle finger before tilting it to the side. He strikes the match against the upturned edge. Angling the match downward, he allows the shaft to become combustible. He turns the cock one half-turn. He watches the blue flame belch to life. He brings the match close to his face to extinguish it. Absently, he holds it to his nostrils to check for smell. There is none. He discards it. He lowers the tall blue flame under the pot. He places the matchbox with its faded design, illegible now, inside the crate.

The needles lie alongside the matches. They are stainless steel, in the kind of package sold at curbsides by blind street peddlers. He opens the paper flap. There, threaded in the red felt, are three needles. He pulls out the smallest. He closes the packet and places it back inside the crate. He finds the spool of very fine thread on the dresser top alongside the mirror. Holding it fast with his three free fingers, he unravels a length of thread and breaks it with his left hand. He places the spool back on the dresser before inserting the thread in the needle's eye. He drops thread and needle in the water. He listens for the faint sound as they strike the metal bottom.

In the crate he gropes for a cartridge of razor blades. He removes one, replacing the cartridge. This, too, he drops in the water. The last item on the dresser, the scissors, he lets slide into the water. Small bubbles begin to form at the edges of the pot.

He props the mirror, balancing it carefully on the dresser top. He stands leaning his weight against the dresser, adjusting the mirror's angle against the wall. There are specks and veins of streaking where the silver has become detached from the reverse side. The glass is thick. At the top a flower is etched. He passes his right hand in front of it, checking for distortion perhaps, or to remove a speck of dirt from its surface. He places the enamel basin on the wireback chair. He tips the galvanized tin bucket over it, filling it with the last of the water. From the crate he pulls out the towel. He lifts it carefully between thumb and index finger and flicks it open, waving it, now back, now forward. He arranges it like a drape over the chairback.

He returns to the crate where he searches in its recesses for a faded plastic soap dish. This he places on the chair beside the water bowl. Then, kneeling before the chair he removes the brown soap from the dish and drops it in the water. He lathers both hands, then returns it to the dish. Raising hands to face, he lathers his temples, and working downward, pressing his eyes shut against the sting, he covers the skin below his eyesockets, moving downward to the chin. Still pressing his eyes shut tight, he lowers his hands into the water once more, rinsing them until the lather is dissolved in the water. Then, cupping water in both hands and inclining his face forward to meet them, he buries his face in his palms. The water overflows into the washbowl. He repeats this gesture until at last he is able to open both eyes. He lifts the towel off the chairback, pats it to his face, then brusquely towels his hands. He replaces the towel, now wrinkled and somewhat damp, on the chairback. He moves back to the dresser. Craning his face forward, he examines it in the mirror. He touches his right cheek, then moves his hand downward toward the mouth, spreading the skin, smoothing it out with his fingers.

The water is boiling now. Judging by the bell clock of the Bomfim, some twenty minutes have passed. He turns the cock until the blue jet sinks down lifeless. He takes a needle from the water and fits it to the syringe. Extracting the plunger, he fills it with procaine. Then spreading the skin just above his mouth, he infuses procaine under the surface. Almost immediately, he feels the area grow numb. With the needle still below the skin, he rotates it slightly, changing its angle. Again, he injects a small amount of procaine into the adjacent area until it, too, is numb. He repeats the process until the tissues surrounding his mouth are entirely numb, before finally extracting the needle. With his finger he taps the area to assure himself that there is no sensation anywhere. Using tweezers, he removes the razor blade from the water. With his fingers he grasps the raised white tissue above and to the right of his mouth. Carefully bending the blade with the constant pressure of thumb and forefinger he lifts off the scar tissue. With his fingers he applies pressure to stem the bleeding. Placing the blade aside, he lifts the needle and thread from the boiling water with the tweezers. He stitches the incision closed with the needle and the very fine thread as best he can, tying the knots one at a time the way he remembers seeing Cardoso do it when, as a boy, he was first apprenticed.

At last, he lets the needle drop. The sterile water is already cold. The red has long diffused, tinting it to rust. He lies down on the cot. The washbasin is still on the chair. He lacks strength to empty it. He will not need it now. Let it sit. It will still be there tomorrow. He shuts his eyes. He can hear a ringing in his ears.

HE IS WANDERING the streets outside. It is dark, no moon, only the kerosene lights glow red in the doorways. The windows are shut tight against the night air. Something is different, uncanny. No trace now of cobblestones, only the lightness of this feeling, his feet barely touching, effortless, like riding a bus, or flying, skimming over the surface quickly, like a dragonfly over water, yes, and feeling what? Some kind of freedom. And then panic. Touching. Touching to make sure. Why isn't the handkerchief there? Why is his face exposed? Someone has died. And, sharp, with that knowing, row upon row of dimly powered lamps swing naked from wires overhead, bright streets (dark only a moment ago) fill with walkers, all solemn, hatted, in a ceremony closed to him, all with handkerchiefs over their faces. And the signs painted red over the doorways: "Moved," "Closed," "For Sale," "Deceased."

He was about to enter the picture show, a room plush, velvety, wine-dark like the soul, and there to take his seat. He was supposed to be there. He had been called. Something there, a welling cloud, a balloon of blue air, now bulging, now concave: eyes, brows, cheekbones, a vast blue Madonna with sad eyes, pulsating, breathing mercy at him, her sad smile, blue lips, skin now pulsing, throbbing with light, each cell opening like a pore, and in each pore, each cell, a face, hundreds of faces, each throbbing, pulsing with its own light.

THE KEROSENE IS SMOKING in the lamp. Before the mirror he is examining his unbandaged face. The first cotton stitches have turned dark, stained with blood. A look comes over him, perhaps of satisfaction. Carefully he avoids a smile. If he were to smile—too early. Cautiously, he fingers the lip. Nothing. He remembers touching it, his mouth, yet he remembers feeling nothing.

What could have happened? He tries to think. He had worked quickly as Cardoso had once showed him, boiling the needle, immersing the thread in the boiling water before use. The razor, sterile. The incisions, clean. The knots, the matching of skin to skin—closing the wound, the gauze, the tape. Could it be the procaine? He tries to think.

It is after all his first attempt. What could have gone wrong? Over the basin, he tries to remember. The wound is closed. He feels the nausea rising, the faintness, and much later, a kind of numbness beyond just his mouth.

A CYCLOPS MOON breathes its light of pewter on the slope. The night wind sighs, and the tall grass weaves with the sway of a somnambulist. Even with the light to ease his task, he moves slowly down the row. He bends beside a young tree, letting the water flow over the bucket's rim, gradually soaking the base, letting the furrowed area contain the water all around, preventing it from overflow.

What could have gone wrong? He had bent his whole effort. He had given it thought, gathered the tools he would need. He had not foreseen this deadening. He imagined rather some coming back to life, some traveling from very far to get it back, not just his face, but his whole life—work he could count on, a place to call his, cronies, a woman perhaps. But not this numbing.

He goes over it again from beginning to end. It must be the nerves, a numbing of the nerves. Could there have been something he overlooked? Could he have bruised one by mistake, or severed it without realizing? It was possible. But it was not possible to go one like this without knowing better, without knowing what he must do.

Back at the pump, he lets the pail drop with a clatter. He turns the spigot. The water drums against the bottom of the bucket. It casts a chilly spray against his hand. He withdraws it absently. He is thinking of the pictures in the waiting area, nineteen in all. He barely hears the spilling of the water as the bucket fills. He is reviewing the pictures, trying to remember the words he once labored to pronounce, and the colors—red for arteries, blue for veins, and for the nerves, yellow. He tries to remember.

The water flows over the edge before he has time to switch buckets. He spills some of the overflow into its twin and moves it under the tap. He must find more pictures, ones he can study. But where? Not here, certainly. Perhaps in a place where they had hospitals, libraries, a medical center. In the district capital. He had only one day free of carrying water. And most of his small savings were spent. A trip to the Capital was out of the question. It would require time and money. He had neither. But to the provincial capital, that was another matter.

At last the bucket is full.

BERNICE ZAMORA

An
Isle
of
Sorrow

A certain sadness draws our sadness
Seven leagues undertide. Very often
Voices without song accompany down
The journey where ages, too, are forgotten.
Crustacean basins form the bed to lie in
Before the dream descends to regions
Known by drowned men. Tobacco fields
Lie fallow. After lunch, sadness lurks
About this Chinese chore. They're going
To attend this wedding, this life of sorrow.

And these are the best years
To cope the thirteen final years,
Not too long for final closure.
On the mantle, touchstones,
An Indian statue bonewhite,
Other trinkets to get Manhattan back.

I Have No Companions

I have no companions to treasure
the strength of my wings,
but inside myself I am married:
an androgynous angel
requires my solitude;
my flesh of light
is hastening over the Spirit
and moving towards a voice in the Sun
where I am lying with open body
to be devoured by the unknown.

A lost city offers me a dwelling
with some exotic lands for my flesh
enraptured in the flowing of things.
It may be wise to obey without knowing
the shape of the tree
that commands illumination,
but I am not the Buddha;
I am just a woman
who balances herself
between two columns.

CARMEN TAFOLLA

Chencho's Cow

I T   A L L   B E G A N   when Chencho's cow kicked over
a pot of beans. The very pot of beans that Chencho had
so painstakingly prepared the night before for the Amados' baby's celebration, selecting the beans with care,
cooking them on a low fire for hours, with salt, chile, and
bacon, then putting in the *tomate, cilantro,* onions, and
more bacon near the end, with, of course, the crowning
touch—a can of beer—to make them *frijoles borrachos,* little drunk beans that he would ladle up into small cups
that people would down like chocolate syrup only better,
not leaving even a teaspoonful of juice at the bottom, and
always going back for more.

It was a special occasion. Elena and Javier Amado had
given birth to a round-cheeked boy whom they named
Carlos Javier after both their fathers; and Chencho, their
neighbor, was invited to the gathering at the house after
the baptism. In fact, he was on the way to the party with
the aromatic pot of beans cradled in potholders when he
heard the cow "moo" loudly and decided to make certain

she still had enough water, since he didn't know how late the party would keep him.

It was for being in a rush (as problems usually are) that he laid the pot down so close to her, thinking just to run the hose a minute and continue on his way. But the smell of those delicious drunk beans must have made the cow more energetic than usual, and when Chencho turned around to pick up the hose, she followed him, kicking over the beans and all their *jugo* on the thirsty dirt. Chencho found himself in a true quandary. He wanted to go to the party but he wanted to take a pot of beans with him. He thought about making up some quick *papa con huevo,* or squeezing some juice into a large *galón* bottle, but that wasn't what he wanted to take. He wanted to take a pot of beans. Worse than that (the truth had to be told) he wanted to take *that* pot of beans—the very pot he made with young Carlos Javier Amado in mind and that now lay flavoring the red sandy dirt. He stared at it, he *wished* it back into the pot, he even thought about scooping up what he could but one look at the cow (and one smell) changed his mind. There was simply nothing that could be done.

The party was as pleasurable as imagined. The townspeople were happy to congratulate (and toast) the young child. Everyone understood about the beans, and they all agreed with Chencho that it was a terrible shame. Chencho took his accordion and played for the party and even promised the young couple a replacement pot of beans for the next Sunday round of visitors. Everyone went home feeling good. Everyone except Chencho.

Every day for a week, he would go out in the barn and stare at the floor, jealously remembering that pot of beans. It got to the point where he began to neglect his fields, and he even shouted angrily at his cow one day. He apologized to her, but still it bothered him—it even bothered him that it bothered him.

One morning, as Chencho was standing in the barn heaving one of his now-customary sighs, someone said, "It doesn't have to happen that way, y'know." Behind him stood an *avena*-faced Anglo, a man dressed formally and all in black like one of those *protestante* ministers, hat coolly in hand. The man pointed to where Chencho's beans had by now (Chencho was sure) fertilized and strengthened the ground with their nutrients. "Such a waste and all for no necessary reason," said the stranger.

Chencho was startled a bit and also a little embarrassed, as if someone had caught him without his clothes on. "My beans?" Chencho verified, his discomfort not permitting any more eloquent a response than that. "Mm-hm," the stranger nodded and looked coolly at the rim of his hat.

"You heard about my beans?" Chencho asked.

"Mm-hm."

A moment of silence passed between them, their wondering eyes missing each other's intentionally.

"Hate to see you feelin' so bad, m'friend."

Funny the way the gringos, especially this kind that traveled through and appeared from nowhere, leaving also into nowhere, liked to call you "my friend" even though they had never laid eyes on you before, and you didn't even know their name. He felt irritated, and embarrassed, that this stranger should know so much about him. He tried to retract from that intimacy, awkwardly, but in a definite retreat.

"I'm alright." His embarrassment and the mutual silence belied his attempt. Chencho took a few steps to the side, and then—thinking better—to the front. The gringo looked away politely.

"It's just that . . . they were for a very special fiesta . . . in the home of my young neighbors . . . the baby boy was named after his two grandfathers—very fine men, very well-respected. . . ." Chencho realized he was rambling and stopped.

"Sure, nothin' the matter with that. Just bein' proper. Anyone could understand that." Chencho relaxed. The man continued, cautiously, "All the same, it do prove a bother, given everythin'." Chencho's brows came together as he studied the talkative gringo. "An' the most bothersome part comes down to just one thing—" Chencho was caught. No one had talked to him about it with such concern since the day after the party, as if everyone else had forgotten or worn out the interesting part of it, and Chencho had had only himself to talk it over with. "Just one thing, m'friend, at the root of it all—causing you all this heartache—" The gringo held the moment, letting Chencho hunger for an answer. "Passion! Jus' plain passion!"

¡Gringo entremetido! Chencho thought, I knew he was sticking too far into my private feelings!

"Now don't go backin' off, m'friend. This is a problem common to the majority of human bein's that inhabit this planet! An to darn near all of the animals! Why that cow of yours just got so excited by the smell o' those beans that she jus' had to kick up her heels an' dance across the floor behind you, kickin' over those special beans o' yours. You'd a thought she would've stepped over logically, or waited till you got the water filled an' was out o' the way, but she jus' got so filled up with passion." Chencho was listening again. "Passion's what did it! Why people go near all their lives gettin' their feelings hurt or broodin' over things, cause o' the trouble that passion causes'm. . ."

By the time he cleared the dishes off the lunch table, Chencho was feelin' pretty good. The gringo had brought in a couple of bottles of elixir from behind the panels of his truck (to cleanse the body after eating, he said), and Chencho was feeling more relaxed than he'd been in a week, with the drone of the gringo's voice putting him just a little (but not too much) to sleep. It never occurred to him to ask what could be done about it, it just somehow made more sense for this whole incident to have had some reason. But the gringo was on his way to some special road, "If only they didn't have their hearts gettin' in the way all the time, *so* much could be accomplished. . . ."

Chencho didn't remember having really thought about it a lot. In fact, he didn't really remember how it all happened. But his cow seemed to be doing fine, and the gringo reassured him that she was actually doing better than she ever had before. Even the scar where her heart had been taken out didn't seem to bother her. And the gringo was sure to point out that she would never again moo at him crossly when Chencho was late to feed or milk her. In fact, she would never again moo at him at all. There was simply no reason to do so.

There was still the matter of Chencho staring at that special spot in the barn and savoring not only the memory of the beans but of the whole *celebración* as he had envisioned it, but the gringo had an idea that he said would take care of that too. It wasn't that Chencho had so much confidence in the gringo—he was a curious sort, that did too much talking and not enough waiting—but it was just that the man had a way of getting him to agree without asking his opinion.

"Passion! M'friend, without our hearts we could get so much more done, and with so much less pain. Now I wouldn't recommend this to ya' if I didn't happen to have seen it work so many times. If we weren't so emotional, we'd have lots more space for being logical. Why the proof o' that's women, ain't it? Get so emotional they don't have an ounce o' logic in'm! Now that's one that a good man like you can really understand, can't ya?" he said, laughing and elbowing Chencho. Chencho didn't, but he laughed anyway, from the mouth outwards, as they say in Spanish, but enough to keep from looking too unmasculine to the gringo.

THIS TIME, Chencho insisted on taking the night to think about it. He would have put it off much longer but the gringo said he had appointments to keep in another town and would have to be leaving this town "sooner than I'd like, m'friend." Chencho talked about it plenty with his neighbors, and some of the things Nilo said got him so upset that he spent the whole night struggling with his pillow and by morning was ready to give it a try, just to get rid of this problem. He went out to the barn, where the cow was just standing, looking very peaceful and unconcerned. "You'd be considered quite a man to have that kind of calm and strength in every situation." Chencho turned to look at the gringo, and something about the man's absoluteness, stark black and white against the brown of the barn, made Chencho want to trust him, want to really make his "m'friend" expression a reality. He was a little nervous about the cutting part, but the gringo explained that the reason the wound had healed so rapidly on the cow, (in fact, it was not even like a wound at all) was that nothing really biological had been removed, only the emotional mass, the heart itself, and without the bother of this too-emotional muscle in its chest, the body could proceed with even greater health, allowing the brain to take over the functions previously so poorly supervised by the heart.

MAYBE IT WAS Marta's grandfather, the one with the weak heart, that did it first, after Chencho, or maybe it was *la rica,* the one who was always so scared of someone stealing the blue tile birdbath that she'd bought in Mexico and placed so precisely in the perfect shady spot in her garden. No one seemed to remember how it had all happened, but they did recall that there were long lines in front of Chencho's house and that everyone went in very envious and excited and admiring how well Chencho and the others seemed to be doing and came out looking very happy, or maybe it was strong, or in control, they weren't certain which. At any rate, by the time three suns had set, there wasn't a normal-brained person over the age of ten that hadn't had his or her heart removed by the kind gringo who brought them the science of "depassionization," as he called it. Chencho's mother had been one of the last to agree, and most of those three days she ranted and raved (quite passionately, proving the gringo's point) against the whole idea, saying that if God had meant people to not struggle for anything he would have given women "labor thoughts" instead of labor pains. The strangest thing of all was that the reason she probably gave in and had it done was because of passion itself! She just couldn't stand to see everyone else in such a predicament and her not right in there with them, with her hands in the *masa,* so to speak.

Chencho's mother had made certain, before placing herself defiantly in that line, however, that her retarded niece, Eva, would not be touched. The gringo agreed, emphatically, stating that it really wouldn't work well on the mentally unfit or on children under ten, because with as little as they'd accumulated up top, they wouldn't have anything left to lean on.

It wasn't until weeks after the gringo left, that they realized something was missing. At first, they thought they were just forgetting things, making a mistake or two, or having a dull day. But the pattern was noticeably repeated. Their thinking process no longer seemed as sharp, and the reasons for thinking things out were not known. Many things left a taste of not having been tasted. Chencho discovered that he no longer remembered how to make beans. This was the case with numerous things: they had to look elsewhere to find what had once been inside of them. Chencho contacted a cousin in a neighboring city and made clear the level of his need. The necessary papers were sent promptly. Chencho would focus all of his attention following the directions with great care. Each step was outlined elaborately. Cleaning the beans required spreading them on the table, removing the stones, removing the beans that were shriveled more than twice as much as the majority, eliminating those that had a very dark color—correction, those that had an unnaturally dark color. (He had wondered what was unnatural and had been told to remove those that looked burnt and reddish, while leaving those that were dark in the same shade as the dark spots on light beans.) It seemed so complex. He had first learned to clean the beans as a child but he had not learned with his head. He had learned with his heart, while watching his grandmother do that which had later become integrated into his view of life. Now, it was integrated into nothing more than the piece of paper he studied so thoroughly, stumbling through the applications.

"Wrinkles that come with life, wrinkles from rubbing against other beans, wrinkles from wilting under the sun—alright. Wrinkles of petrified stone—no." He worked at it repeatedly, adding precisely measured amounts of ingredients at precisely timed stages. Chencho found that every time he cooked beans, he had to follow the written instructions again. But follow as he did, they never seemed to have the same taste as before. It was as if there was some ingredient missing, but he had no idea what to add.

Chencho and the others would sit in the evenings, trying to piece together those things that their hearts could no longer provide. Eva, the retarded thirty-five year old, began to play a crucial role. She was the one they turned to for lessons in how to cuddle babies and how to help the older children play. They listened carefully as she and the little children laughed, trying to imitate the sound.

They tried to make lists of what it was they had lost, what they had had, and what had been said in those days of the gringo's visit. They tried to piece together old conversations, but somehow every conversation had something important missing between the lines. The eight and nine year olds were brought in to listen and respond, but even their responses were difficult to comprehend. The teenagers just took notes. Chencho's mother proposed they go over every event and every conversation from the day of the gringo's arrival to the day of his departure. Chencho remembered his climbing into the truck with some salutation, what was it? The children offered possible expressions until the right one was found. "Goodby, my friend," the gringo had said, as he folded the worn dollar bills into his pocket. "And then what?" asked Jorge, as the Amados' baby began to cry, and the adults turned to stare at him. "He wants his bottle," said a bright-eyed seven year old.

Chencho thought carefully and found the information as best he could through his passionless brain. "And then he told me how fortunate we would be—to be able to work longer days in the sun, without feeling upset, and to bring home paychecks of any amount at all, without wanting to cry." "What?" asked Elena, thoroughly confused, "Without wanting to cry?" "Yes, that's what he said." "Is that all?" asked his mother, whom people somehow sensed should be regarded as a leader, although they were not certain why. "No," said Chencho slowly, "there was something more . . . something . . . like that, like what that child just did." "He laughed?" asked the seven year old. "Yes, that was it. He laughed. He laughed," Chencho verified, "and then he drove off." In the distance, Chencho's cow could be heard moving around the barn, her bell dangling against the trough as she searched for food, but everyone knew that she would never again bother to moo.

ELIANA SÚAREZ RIVERO

North from the River, South Inside

(Florida, 1961–Arizona, 1980)

I

the way it all began   as they say
in old tales   was surprising:
suddenly I had no clay under my feet
but sand was holding what I was

I clutched a few and carefully tended
myths and entered
into this territory of submersion:
north from my childhood
and from my early stories of each day

in the land where I grew (neon-lighted
showcase for underdevelopment)   where we went
to church every Sunday and subtracted
smiles from the boys around the park
and the teacher told us that the Blessed
Virgin would cry if we so much as had
an impure thought (let alone play footsie)
and we merrily danced and forgot
that others were not invited to our clubs:
                              suddenly
that reality was no more
than a crushing distance   the presence was
walls that shouted "you're in America now and have to
speak American"   and how does one learn
to untalk all the past
        another world would have to be forgotten
        and the journey somehow erased
to be able to eat breakfast every morning and
go to school and
pay the bus fare and
read the messages of alienation:
            seven or eight times January came around
before I could walk into a room and feel
I wasn't really from another planet
        my hair was brown   as it should be
        instead of green
and the accents of the tongue were forgiven
by well-meaning hostesses who never
failed to ask "how do you like it here?"   and then
the act of gratitude   of intense
repetition of thanks   (which were really sincere and
wagging-of-the-puppy-tail-like)   and then the cute

and condescending references to talent
and land of opportunity for all
        but I couldn't   (I didn't know the words)
recite the pledge of allegiance   and so
they made me cross the water
    I spent a foreign day in a colorful sunny
    marketplace and bought a big hat and straw purses
    that had embroidery all over and said

NASSAU, BAHAMAS   and the stewardess
insisted on my drinking Bloody Marys at
seven-thirty in the morning   because
the Caribbean was so blue   and
I was coming back forever   to stripes
        and amber waves of grain

I I

south from the present: it remained
underground for so long   deeply tucked away
in the recesses of the soul   I never
thought it would begin to surface
        nevertheless it slowly filtered   through
recoiling   at the mentioning of impositions
of phrases that made fun
    of the other part of me   the early errors
sunlight in the avenues   a novel that
brings back   the setting for a previous love
living on a strange (and worse than that, indifferent)
street   full of faces that had never
    existed in my dreams

smell of sea port   and grease from shipyards
and twenty pounds of laundry taken to the corner
      the old lady would say that tablecloths were badly
folded   and fixed cabbages and onion rings
for supper   while one could hear the clatter
      of dusk and dishes above the din of rotting
      apartment houses
María the neighbor refused to eat while her daughters
were still in jail   and then would sit on the
   front steps and listen to short-wave radio
   for news in her own language   and I would try
to do my homework   (it was chemistry or math because
I never wrote a line that was unnecessary in those days)
and then the jars of peanut butter and the boxes
of rolled oats   U.S. DEPARTMENT OF AGRICULTURE—
SURPLUS COMMODITIES   I learned to read them
   carefully
every fifth of the month
and liked their cardboard flavor because
it came from the Midwest and heartland of the country
(it was free anyhow and it made for good cookies)
   at the library I used to borrow Mozart records and
   my old aunt's recordplayer almost got me in trouble
with scratches on *Eine Kleine Nachtmusik*   what the hell
was I doing listening to German music in the middle of
Florida?   well I was an expert on the other kind of
música bailable   and culture was the name of the game
"education for the future citizen"   and lots
of peanut butter cookies for the swallowing

III

years make it seem so unreal but
it existed: Miss Miller who at fifty-five
swore never to rent her nice one-bedroom   apartment
to another Cuban: the tenant had strange ways of
celebrating hurricanes with a party and
her strong coffee made stains in the sink
   the upstairs neighbor   (very proper high school
   administrator)   had a visitor
   every Thursday evening   and my living room rafters
   would screech with the jolts of the bed
   and middle-aged white Anglo-Saxon
   passionate Protestants making love
   over my head
another uncle of mine was married
to a Puerto Rican lady who shopped at Jordan Marsh
and scolded me for studying too much (most of all *Spanish*
   of all idiotic things)   and she recited
every time I was her captive audience   "marry a doctor,
nice, Latino parents but American ways"   and then
proceeded to engage in solid conversation for two years
reciting   all the wonderful values she had learned
as a bicultural   and I was still
chewing cookies made with oats from the USDA

I V

and all is oh so far beyond
my present   north from the river
where I live   and suddenly exist in memories
where sand made its castles   one day for me
to come and play   this is
another land of plenty   where I reap and am reaped
where I deal in my words   and forget
that I ever ate surplus commodities   and I look at the
     very
beginning of Latin America out of my kitchen window
(a little town with dirty streets called Naco, Sonora,
     Mexico,
where we cross the border and get sad and feel angry and
     buy
Bacardí Carta Oro but it doesn't taste the same) and still
the two circles surround me   the dual love-and-
     hate
relationship   my languages   the mother that I
     recognize
as real   legitimate and splendid   and the surro-
     gate
the tongue that lets me be two times   the person
     that I am
the presence of the territory   that engulfs me
and all the memories   of southern places
     inside
     hurting

MARY GUERRERO MILLIGAN

Lotería: La Rosa

GRANDMA'S HOUSE is now a barbershop. I drive past wondering if I should take my son in for a haircut. I decide not to because he is very particular about his hair and this doesn't look like his kind of barbershop—a barbershop on a downtown side street with a red and white pole in front. And yet I haunt the house. My spirit has walked past the barbershop pole through the shop's walls past the hair clippings and scissors to my grandmother's kitchen.

I return again and again to her kitchen as a little girl. Standing in front of Grandma's kitchen table, I see her sitting with her two neighbors, little piles of pennies and pinto beans in front of them with *lotería* game boards. It looks like a grown-up birthday party, but Grandma says that Mexican bingo is not a children's game.

Playing for pennies, each player has three or four game boards and a handful of pinto beans for markers. The deck of cards is in the center of the table, face down. Grandma turns them over slowly one at a time. I love looking at the different *lotería* cards. Each picture gives color to my black-and-white memories. I stare at each beautiful picture, as real to me now as then. The brightly colored *sandía* still makes my mouth water, so perfectly ripe and juicy. Even now, whenever I pass a fruit vendor selling watermelons I wonder if it could possibly be as sweet as *la sandía* in Grandma's kitchen.

I try to be patient as I wait for number 48, *la chalupa,* to be called. Will she be called this game or will I have to sit through another until I see her again? Lovely and graceful in her narrow boat, I long to squeeze between her fruits and flowers and join her in her travels. Where is she going? Will she ever have room for me? Her card, more than any other, is alive for me. I can hear the gentle ripples as her boat glides through the water. Once when I touched her picture, my finger came away moist.

I often walk by the San Antonio River and sometimes, when the water is especially calm, I can see the faint ripples of a narrow boat that has recently passed. Where is *la chalupa* going? Is anyone riding with her? Will she ever let me join her?

In Grandma's house, I am stripped of all that time has given me, able to revisit my earliest memories. Today I am waiting for a new *lotería* game to begin. It is a hot, sticky afternoon, but Grandma is refreshed from her nap and ready for a long session of bingo. Anticipation makes everyone silent. Except for the steady hum from the fan in the corner and the shuffling of the cards, the room is quiet and still. Pete in his tank-top undershirt and his wife An-dréa in her brown print housedress watch my Grandmother carefully as she shuffles the cards—once, twice, three times. Placing the cards face down in the middle of the table signals the start of a new game.

The first card called is:

LA ROSA

Waking up heavy with sleep in my grandmother's bedroom I hear the sound of bells. The room is cold, but I am warm deep under the covers. The house is dark except for two candles flickering on the altar in the next room. I can see Grandma's silhouette. She is kneeling in front of the candles, as still as her statues on the altar. While the shadows dance around the altar, I begin to doze, when I again hear the sounds that woke me up.

I know what it is: clip clop clip clop jingle jingle jingle. Wide awake, I throw off the covers, my heart pounding with excitement. *"Quién viene? Santa Claus? Con reindeer?"* Christmas Day is almost two weeks away, and I don't understand how this can be happening. Shivering with cold, I try to see out the window by the bed. The window is foggy from the cold, and I wipe it with my sleeve, making my arm feel wet and chilled but I don't care. I will see Santa tonight.

"No no, mija. Son los caballeros. Van a cantarle a la Virgen," answers my grandmother. Now that I have rubbed the mist from the window I can see the horses clearly. Two rows of black and silver riders wearing huge sombreros ride slowly past us carrying guitars and trumpets. I hear their soft strumming intermingled with the horses' hoof beats against the paved street.

While we watch the riders shrink into the night, Grandma explains that today is the day we sing *las Mañanitas* to *la Virgen de Guadalupe*. Before sunrise the riders will serenade *la Virgen* in front of the church. She tells me about how special today is for *la familia* in Mexico. As I begin to get sleepy I listen to her stories about visiting *la Virgen* with candles and roses. She reminds me that spring will soon be here and that her garden will be filled with many beautiful roses and if I want and if I am good, I may choose any of her roses to give to *la Virgen* and to my teacher at school. Under the covers again, I drift back to sleep as the dawn begins to creep behind the office buildings and the church bells begin to ring, thinking about the sleeping rose bushes outside the bedroom window that will soon be filled with roses, and I am not disappointed that it is still almost two weeks away from Christmas.

The roses are long gone, yet their scent fills my mind. I walk through her garden, down her street, trying to recapture my lifeblood, but I stand in the middle of a parking lot. I am a barbershop ghost, searching.

Downtown was Grandma's neighborhood. We walked everywhere: to her work, to the Cathedral, to eat at *El Bohemio,* to visit the local *curandera* or to shop at *El Mercado.* An impatient walker, she refused to acknowledge traffic lights, racing across before the light flashed "WALK." She'd never wait and would walk against the light regardless of the traffic. Asking her why we were risking our lives, pointing to the red "DON'T WALK," she'd remind me in Spanish, *"Yo soy mexicana y . . .* I—don't—read—English."

On bad weather days we'd take the shopper's special. Paying a nickel, we'd ride one of the slow-moving buses as it crawled its way through town. It was usually very entertaining listening to the passengers on the crowded ride: fast-talking *viejitas,* loud-talking *muchachos,* English, Spanish, crying babies, giggling school girls in their Catholic school uniforms. And as soon as we were off the bus, Grandma would argue about how much faster it would have been to walk.

I loved our walks together. Grandma was not a silent walker. She talked as fast as she walked. No light conversations or playful chatter, instead a steady catechism about the way I should live my life. While I explored her neighborhood, she'd explore my heart. Even now the noise, the color, the smell of downtown can take me back to those walks.

Another cold, early morning. It is a little after sunrise when we enter *El Bohemio*. My mother and I have joined Grandma an hour earlier to help her finish cleaning the office buildings across the street. Now all three of us are ready for breakfast. The cooking smells remind me of my hunger while the mariachi music from the jukebox keeps me awake.

This morning Chorte is our waiter. He is my favorite as well as a friend of my grandmother. With an easy smile and a gentle manner, he shares his daily story with us. They are usually funny and I eagerly await his new tale. I order my regular *El Bohemio* breakfast: one *barbacoa taco* and one *chorizo con huevo taco.* As we wait for our tacos, we sip our coffee. I drink some of Grandma's coffee in her small glass creamer. She always drinks sugary coffee with lots of milk. It tastes warm and sweet.

But this morning I don't like Chorte's story. It's about catching a pigeon in the park for last night's supper, and I can't believe any of it. That he was able to or that he would want to or that he, my dear friend, could ever do such a thing. I try not to cry or show the pain that I feel inside but Grandma senses it and doesn't approve. After he leaves, Grandma is angry with me. She points out that the pigeons in the park are food to him, not pets, and that in Mexico where she and Chorte are from people sometimes have to do worse. But what is worse than eating the park pigeons that come to you because you will feed them? She reminds me that *barbacoa* is a cow and *chorizo* is a pig and that farmers feed their animals lovingly right up to the time of their slaughter.

We finally get our tacos, and now I am mad at Grandma for telling me that my wonderful breakfast might be some little girl's pet so I begin to eat my taco like a *gringa*. I take big bites right down the middle of the taco, eating it like a sandwich until it is split in half. Grandma watches me with growing displeasure. Telling me that I am eating it all wrong, she shows me the *mexicana* way. She squeezes one end tight with her fingers to keep the juices in and bites from the opposite end. I laugh to myself as she demonstrates the proper way.

I try to retrace our walks: to the Cathedral, *El Bohemio,* back to her home. But like a puzzle with missing pieces, the picture is incomplete. Standing in front of her bedroom window, amid the dead rose bushes, I knock against her window, hoping to wake her up, but my hand goes through the wall.

The Singing Antelope

DURING DAYLIGHT, I can dream I see what I see—my house stands still between rows of rooted poplars. At night, if I open my eyes, I feel the earth move, and shortly, my house and I float between treetops. It's the moon—slipping from cloud to cloud. And the stars. But it takes much longer to see stars.

I know he never saw them, although—and I have forgiven him everything because of it—he pretended. He never cared about what was real as I did—only whether things were going as he wished. Lying came easily to him.

He's suffering now, there on that narrow hospital bed—perhaps most because there's no way to maneuver. When we come into life, one tube is all we need. When we die—he looks like a bug caught in a web. This is not how I've known him, how any of us have. My younger sister pleads when she visits, scolds him as if he's in a mad, fatal sulk. As eldest daughter, childless, I watch around the clock. He doesn't know how my presence buffers him, how I give him permission to be mortal. I doubt he'd want that from me, but it hardly matters. For years now, we've had to slip each other what we have to give.

When I was seventeen, his silhouette loomed in my doorway. The brightness of the light behind him darkened his face, his body, and rested in his own sense of himself as a figure not quite divine, but certainly not simply human. As a consequence he trusted himself to me and allowed me my own head. I believe I loved him more than anyone ever had, and so, inevitably, we dashed one another's hearts.

I hated him for lying to me—and, then, it was another woman, too. Mother had been right about that—the only victory life gave her, I'm afraid. I first saw the antelope during my customary escape from their mutual dismemberments. I lay on the garage roof watching for falling stars, dreaming of a young woman of my own. Nights in the valley towns were rather quiet then. We had automobiles and planes, of course, but not so many of them that darkness ceased belonging to itself. And our house was on the edge of the mesa stretching miles toward the mountains. I had more sky than I could see.

The creature simply appeared although it was so distant and dim I assumed it wasn't where I saw it. I'd always thought we made the constellations up, grouped the stars in familiar shapes so we could recognize them, like faces. And this creature was not quite an antelope, either. For one thing, it had five legs, two coming out of its left haunch. And its tail had the sweep of a comet.

The cry of my parents' rage broke through the house, swelled into the night. I thought perhaps they might murder each other, and I felt the oddest peace. The urge to throw myself between them or to besiege God with prayers simply was gone. I was willing for even death to happen—I mean, even though it was they who were rending each other, I took what they were doing on myself. I can't explain. Only, for once, I both cared and didn't care with all my heart. And then I was free. Death felt perfectly inevitable; I, inexplicable; the world, absolutely open.

Getting ready for my journey was innocent. I took some water and a jacket. There was no moon and no way to know where I was going except that flickering body of stars that apparently had descended to the desert.

I picked my way through the sagebrush and cactus talking with myself.

Why are you alive now?

I don't know.

Why here?

I don't know.

With these people?

I don't know.

As you are?

I don't know.

Joy seeped into me with the starlight, filling me like my own blood. I could have been anywhere or never, and Lena's face filled my dreams.

Why not?

Oh God—his chest is heaving. If only I could breathe for him. No, no that won't do—not even for a moment. His face is so empty now, except for pain. My lending him my breath would be a violence against all he has been.

He wouldn't forgive me Lena. I was the only child he never hit. My sister tells me he beat her the night he found out. I hadn't spoken to him, myself, in years. We didn't talk, really, until after I was forty and had betrayed Lena. I left her for a younger woman, much as he had Mother.

At first, I asked him whether he'd be pleased if I moved back to town.

"It's too late for that," he said. The next time I saw him, about four years later, we talked like old lovers who no longer needed anything of one another. Finally, he asked me about Lena. And I told him in pieces as we walked the mesa. It was twilight when I told him of the antelope, of walking across the mesa under the stars feeling the ecstasy of my mortality, drawing ever closer to the constellation that had somehow fallen to the earth. I walked all night, and indeed the stars grew larger, softer as I continued. The night was still an hour from dawn when I heard. I'd already seen it fully for some time.

It was taller than any building I had ever seen—tall enough to suck the earth it stood on toward the sky. Mostly, it was darkness. I could see it only by the stars that marked it randomly. Stars outlined its face, its long neck, much longer than any earthly antelope's. There was a star at the tip of one ear, and an arch of stars along a tail that shot from its three hind legs straight toward the heavens. Its hindquarters were lifted, and its body seemed to pour toward its shoulders, a vessel of night. The closer I came, the more it resembled my own soul during the moment before I move. It was drawn into a breath of poise and gazed down into the arroyos far below.

And then I heard it sing. My body folded, and I wept. Its song was eight notes, and they rose like a scale, but the closest scale I had ever heard to the intervals of the antelope's song was a psalm a visiting Greek priest had once sung in our church. And yet this song was as far beyond his as the universe is beyond the sun. The antelope repeated it again and again, this rising call weaving the earth to heaven in strands of longing and love. I then not only knew that I would one moment die, but I knew the moment did not matter, that the meaning of a life is instantaneous, its completion impossible. And I knew, then, that I would choose for love.

He listened to me gravely. "I, too, had a young love, once," he said. She had been beautiful and in love with him, and he had been overwhelmed and grateful. He worshipped her. Parents, fate, time intervened. He did not see her again until they each had raised children. She was still beautiful, and still in love. "I told her I did not want to sleep with her," he said. "I told her what we had was still perfect and that nowhere else did I still have that."

I have learned that loving is an art to be studied and served, so I don't know if I understood him or not. Perhaps he had his own visions. Perhaps, in some way, he even understands mine.

Last night, I held his hand as he fell asleep. Before he drifted off, he told me he'd been dreaming of his father, of trying to swim the river by his childhood home. He smiled. "You're the one who remembers dreams," he said to me. I hold his hand again, and help him dream his death.

CHERRÍE MORAGA

New
Mexican
Confession

Upon reading Whitman fifteen years later. Jemez Springs, 1988

I

There is great joy in the naming
of things that mean no more
than what they are.
Cottonwood in winter's nakedness,
frozen black skeleton
against red rock canyon walls
converging onto this thin river of water
and human activity:
Los Ojos Bar
Hilltop Hotel and Café
the grain and feed shop.

These were the words denied me in any language:
piñón
cañón

arroyo
except as names on street signs,
growing up in California sprawl,
boundaries formed
by neat cement right angles.

2

Like a poet
I have come here to look for god
but make no claim of finding—
the quest, a journey
of righteous and humble men
strangers to their bodies
cartographers to the contour of woman-flesh,
a border between nature and its lover,
man.

I am a woman
who walks by the motherhouse
of the sisters of the precious blood
sleeping beneath the snow
and can as easily see myself there
my body sleeping beneath the silent
smell of fresh pressed linen,
the protection of closed doors
Against the cold
Against the foul breath 'n' beer
talk of Alaskan pipeliners passing through
Against the vibrant death this land is seeing. . .

Who do they pray for? Do they pray for this land?

The sister ventures out into the cold of noon
to play the *campanas.* They sound of tin,
a flat resonance as I pass
no even twelve strikes but a sporadic three strikes here
another two—rest—again three
and I imagine she calls me as I always feared
to join her in her single bed
of aching abstinence.

I am the nun
as I am the Giusewa woman
across the road
who 300 years ago
with mud and straw and hands
as delicate as her descendant's
now scribbling on dead leaves,
walled up the Spanish religion
built templos to enclose his god
while the outer cañón
enveloped and pitied them all.

3

My sin has always been to believe
myself man, to sing a song
of *my*self that inhabited everyone.

I fall to sleep contemplating the body of the poet

Whitman at my age, 100 years ago
and see his body knew the same fragility,
the desire to dissolve the parameters of flesh
and bone and blend with the mountain
the blade of grass
the boy.

I *bleed* with the mountain
the blade of grass
the boy
because my body suffers in its womb.
The maternal blood that courses this frozen ground
was not spilt in violence, but in mourning.

I am everyman more than man.
This is my sin.
This knowledge.

Being Indian,
a Candle,
and So Many
Dying Stars

I LEFT THE PARLOR midway through the video about the Chamula Indian and his dying boy and told Eugenia and David who were sitting in the kitchen having a shot of mezcal that David took from his Buddhist altar to calm their nerves since they had both just been kicked out of a bar down the street for no other reason than that the bartender didn't like their faces and I said, "I can't watch anymore. Is there any mezcal left?"

They both shook their heads. There had only been a tiny bottle of it, the size you buy on airplanes but I don't know any airlines that carry mezcal. I was trying not to cry since I am supposed to be the brave one of the group although they don't know that or seem to think so. "It is moments like this, watching that story about the Chamulas that I know that I am Indian," I said in my own language and not in this one that I am speaking to you now because if I don't, like the Chamulas, my story will be annihilated and not heard.

Eugenia looked up at me flushed with the alcohol she had just had and said, "What are you talking about? Have you ever taken a look at yourself in the mirror?" Eugenia is a bit disrespectful, which sometimes is a very good thing for her as a mix-blood woman, a *mestiza,* to be irreverent. But I've noticed that she is not very discerning about her disrespect, which at that moment was directed at me. If I am not considered the bravest of the group, or the smartest, I am the oldest. And no one seems to want to take issue with that fact. At the very least, it isn't very nice to be ornery with one's elders.

I've decided that Eugenia is an anarchist. This conclusion was drawn one night when she called herself a leftist and later announced that she was giving up her acting career, which consisted of one small but important part in a play, and was leaving the country however she could manage it and as soon as she could, to be an American exile. I didn't understand what that could possibly mean since a person had to have a country—which she claimed she did not have, in order to be in exile. Although she considered herself a leftist I mostly observed her to be frustrated with everything, including my hope, my revolutionary work, and my action. Therefore, it came to my mind and rested comfortably in my private thoughts that she was an anarchist.

I liked her very much and I'm sure my age and my hope granted me saintly patience so I usually did not acknowledge her disrespect with words but always made a gesture as if to slap her upside her head but of course never did.

"*Who* has ever told *you* that you are not Indian?" She asked in disbelief.

"Many people, believe it or not," I said.

"Like who?"

I wished I had been invited to that bit of mezcal because I was still shivering from the video about the Chamula father travelling and travelling on foot with his feverish boy on his shoulders, looking for a doctor and being an Indian there would be no doctor so I had stopped the video halfway, as I said, knowing also that Indians must walk even after death.

"Once in New Mexico I was going to a house blessing ceremony at the Zuñi pueblo and a white woman said to me: 'I don't think the Zuñi are allowing white people to attend this year.' 'I'm not white,' I said. 'To the Zuñi people you are as white as I am.' That's what she said to me. After a moment of recuperation, I said, 'It's true that my people are not Zuñi, but I'm not white.' "

"And it's not true that the Zuñi people would see us as white!" David said in a loud voice. Eugenia said nothing because she was angry at everybody. This little story had served only as one more brick on the wall she was building against a world of nations, to none of which she belonged.

There are things that I am. There are things that I am not. There are also some things that change. For instance, I was not always the oldest of a group. For a long time, I was always the youngest member and very quiet. I listened in order to become a person. Now, in such groups, I do most of the talking.

The young ones are not always listening, however.

"I know that," I said to David and looked at Eugenia, "But that is what she said to me. And in New Mexico, I had another woman, who identifies herself as *nuevomejicana,* also say that I am not Indian. So I asked her, 'Then what am I?' 'Hispanic, of course,' she said, *'we're* Hispanic.' "

Eugenia shook her head because she is from New Mexico and I think she felt ashamed.

Having made my point, which in this case was like being told to tie a double knot one more time, I went on, "When I was in Paris speaking at the Sorbonne I was asked by the students, 'Now that you're here, where do you feel you belong?'

Come to think of it, I don't know what they meant by that question, but what I understood is how I answered so I said, "My spirit belongs to the Americas. I've been there for thousands of years. I'm sure of that now that I'm here."

Eugenia had nothing to say because she had never been to Paris but also because she did not know what to say.

David nodded. "It was like that for dark people in Paris," he added. They went there to get away from not being wanted where they were born, except for the Algerians. The Algerians went there to work as well as to be not wanted there.

"Of course, in Paris, I was not considered an American, either," I said. "I stayed with a French woman who spoke nothing but French. She was a mathematician and was useless with language. So she invited her socialite sister so that she could come and converse with me. She was married to a doctor and they had lived in the United States for many years.

The sister came over while I was in the kitchen helping with the dishes. She stuck her head in the kitchen. We exchanged glances. And then she said very loudly to her sister, 'So where is the American?' She had mistaken me for the maid."

"But she said it in English. . ." David said. "Presumably her sister didn't understand English. So, for whose benefit did she ask that in English?"

"The American's." I said.

"So where did she think the American was?"

"I don't know," I said.

"People love to hate the United States," David said, "like a rich uncle."

"Yeah—rich Uncle Sam!" Eugenia said.

"And like that rich uncle," I said, "they tolerate it and are forced to cater to it, waiting and hoping for the moment he croaks to see if they were left anything in the will."

At that moment, Jorge came in. "How did you like the video?" He asked me in our language, or rather, one of our languages. He had lent me the video. "It was beautiful," I said, "But it made me think too much of my son so I had to stop watching it."

"You have a son?" Jorge asked. Jorge and I really didn't know each other.

"Yes," I said, of course, since I had just mentioned my son.

"Where is he?" he asked, as if at any moment my child would jump out from behind a half-opened door. The others looked uneasy, too. I don't know why. Maybe they weren't uneasy but the acknowledgment of an absent child was in itself an uneasy fact.

"He's with his father," I said.

Jorge nodded. He didn't ask anything more, and I wasn't sure if this was because the question of the absent child was settled with the knowledge that he was with his father or because he didn't care.

There was some silence around the table. David lit the candle that was there and got up to turn off the kitchen light. This increased our solemnity. And with our solemnity our silence was given breadth. While I couldn't see it, I felt the moon over the desert, which were very far away, both desert and moon.

But I couldn't feel the stars, not the ones I slept under as a child. I couldn't feel their rapid oscillation as I always felt them in the desert, even when I didn't look out the door to verify that it was the stars making me tremble. The stars, like the moon in the city with high-rise buildings where these new and old friends had come together like family on the simple basis of sharing rent were city stars. It was a city moon out there surely shining, although well hidden behind layers of smog and not giving any light to the world.

Then David broke the silence and staring without blinking at the candle flame he said, "I'm glad I'm not a father."

Jorge laughed nervously and lit a cigarette.

I stood up straight.

"Come on now, David," Eugenia said with a smile, "Not all children are bad!"

"Children are people," he said. His eyes were transfixed on the flame and I began to stare at it too. "I'm not saying they are not all good or all bad. They are people and they are not innocent simply because they are children."

Out in the city sky there were stars at that moment dying, the sun included. The earth was also said to be dying. And David, who my eyes and therefore my mind told me was across the table from me at that moment, was also dying at that very moment. We were all dying, of course, which is the nature of life. But David already knew about his death. His illness had a name but no cure. It had symptoms but no fixed cause. Each of us was helpless to it but David was helpless most of all.

So, out of compassion for David who knew the name of his death and therefore all his thoughts were following after it, as if following a colon, I said, "Well, I am only responsible for the particular behavior of one child. And he is very self-assured, very loving and very sweet."

Eugenia, out of sense of loyalty for something or someone, nodded but said nothing. Jorge didn't know my son so he nodded as one can only do to a proud mother who has just made such a comment. And David kept staring at the candle flame before it went out and left us in the dark.

Notes
on the
Contributors

Born in Bethesda, Maryland, **Marjorie Agosín** was raised in Chile, the adopted homeland of her Russian and Viennese Jewish grandparents. The family fled from Chile just before the assassination of President Allende, thereby escaping the ensuing military oppression. Agosín studied in the U.S., eventually earning her Ph.D. from Indiana University. A dedicated human rights activist, Agosín has received the Jeanetta Rankin Award in Human Rights, the Good Neighbor Award from the Conference of Christians and Jews, and numerous literary and scholarly awards. All of her works reflect her concern for the abuse of human rights throughout Latin America.

Agosín's poetry includes *Conchalí, Brujas y Algo Más/Witches and Other Things* (Latin American Review Press, 1984), *Women of Smoke* (Red Sea Press, 1988), *Zones of Pain* (White Pine Press, 1988), *Hogueras/Bonfires* (Bilingual Review Press, 1990), *Sargasso* (White Pine Press, 1993), and most recently, *Toward the Splendid City* (Bilingual Review Press, 1994). Her collection of prose poems, *Circles of Madness: Mothers of the Plaza de Mayo* (White Pine Press, 1992), was illustrated with photographs of the mothers of the disappeared and other grim scenes from Argentina. *La Felicidad*, first published in Santiago, is Agosín's first prose collection to be published in English. The story included in this anthology is from *Happiness* (White Pine Press, 1994), translated by Elizabeth Horan. Agosín's latest work is *A Cross and a Star: Memoirs of a Jewish Girl in Chile* (University of New Mexico Press, 1995).

Agosín has been a professor in the Spanish Department of Wellesley College for the past sixteen years. She is also on the advisory board of *Ms.* magazine.

The parents of **Julia Alvarez,** underground opponents of the dictatorship of General Raphael Leonidas Trujillo, were forced to flee the Dominican Republic after their activities became known to Trujillo's secret police. They arrived in New York with their ten-year-old daughter in August 1960.

In 1984, Alvarez published her first collection of poetry, *Homecoming,* which will be reprinted by Dutton NAL in 1996. Her first novel, *How the García Girls Lost Their Accents* (Algonquin, 1991), was received with critical acclaim. Named a "Notable Book" by both *The New York Times* and the American Library Association, it received the PEN Oakland/Josephine Miles Award. Alvarez's second novel, *In the Time of the Butterflies,* was published by Algonquin in 1995. Currently, Alvarez is a professor of literature at Middlebury College in Vermont.

Gloria Anzaldúa's ancestors owned land in South Texas from the early eighteenth century through the early twentieth. By the 1930s, however, racist political and legal maneuvering, combined with the drought of that era, had reduced the family to sharecropping. Anzaldúa was born near the old family lands in Raymondville, Texas. She attended Pan American University at Edinburg, Texas, and received her M.A. from the University of Texas at Austin. She is currently completing her Ph.D. at the University of California at Santa Cruz, where she has lived for several years.

Anzaldúa is the co-editor, with Cherrie Moraga, of the anthology *This Bridge Called My Back: Radical Writings by Women of Color* (Persephone Press, 1981), recipient of the Before Columbus Foundation's American Book Award. *La Frontera/Borderlands: The New Mestiza,* a collection of memoirs, essays, poetry, and folklore, was published by Aunt Lute in 1987. Anzaldúa has also edited *Haciendo Caras/Making Face, Making Soul: Creative and Critical Perspectives by Women of Color* (Aunt Lute, 1990) and is the author of two children's books, *Prietita Has a Friend/Prietita Tiene un Amigo* (Children's Book Press, 1991) and *Prietita Encounters La Llorona* (Children's Book Press, 1995).

• Notes on the Contributors •

Miriam Bornstein is a poet and critic who was born in Puebla, Mexico, to a Mexican mother and a Polish father, and has lived in the United States since 1964. After obtaining her Ph.D. from the University of Arizona, she became assistant professor in the Department of Languages and Literatures at the University of Denver, where she presently teaches Chicano and Latin American literature and culture.

She has published two books of poetry, *Bajo Cubierta/Under Cover* (Scorpion Press, 1976) and *Donde Empieza la Historia/Where the Story Begins* (Spanish Press, 1993). Her poetry has been published in literary magazines such as *Letras Femeninas, Revista Chicano-Riquena* and *Arieto,* and has appeared in national and international anthologies including *Latina Creative Literature: An Anthology of Hispanic Women Writers; Siete Poetas; Nosotras: Latina Literature Today, Chicano Literature Written in Spanish; La Voz Urgente: Antología de Literature Chicano en Español,* and most recently, *Infinite Divisions: An Anthology of Chicana Literature* (University of Arizona Press, 1993). Some of her critical essays have appeared in *Revista Casa de las Americas, Duadernos Americanos, La Palabra,* and *The Denver Quarterly.*

Chicago novelist, poet, editor, and translator, **Ana Castillo** is one of the world's leading Latina voices. She is the author of four collections of poetry, *Otro Canto* (1977), *The Invitation* (1979), *Women Are Not Roses* (Arte Público Press, 1984) and *My Father Was a Toltec* (West End Press, 1988).

Castillo's first novel, *The Mixquiahuala Letters* (Bilingual Review Press, 1986), received an American Book Award from the Before Columbus Foundation and was selected by the National Endowment for the Arts for presentation at book fairs in Frankfurt and Buenos Aires. Following *Sapogonia* (Bilingual Review Press, 1988), it was her *So Far from God* (Norton, 1993) that brought Castillo a national reputation and critical acclaim. Her latest work is *Massacre of the Dreamers: Essays on Xicanisma* (University of New Mexico Press, 1994). A native of Chicago, Castillo has lived, studied, and taught all over the U.S. and Europe. She has received a National Endowment for the Arts fellowship and was recently recognized for "outstanding contributions to the arts" by the National Association of Chicano Studies.

Born in San Antonio, Texas, **Rosemary Catacalos** brings to her poetry elements of both her Mexican and Greek ancestry. Her first book, *As Long As It Takes* (Iguana Press, 1984), was followed by *Again for the First Time* (Tooth of Time, 1984), which received the Texas Institute of Letters Poetry Prize. Catacalos has received four Pushcart Prize nominations and a Special Mention in Pushcart Prize IX. She was awarded a 1985 Dobie Paisano Fellowship by the University of Texas at Austin and the Texas Institute of Letters, was a Stegner Creative Writing Fellow in Poetry at Stanford University from 1989 to 1991, and received a National Endowment for the Arts fellowship in poetry.

A former newspaper reporter and columnist, Catacalos was the literature program director for the Guadalupe Cultural Arts Center from 1986 to 1989, and has served extensively on panels for the National Endowment for the Arts, several state commissions on the arts, and other organizations, including the Council of Literary Magazines and Presses and the Lila Wallace–Reader's Digest Fund. Currently she is the executive director of The Poetry Center and American Poetry Archives at San Francisco State University.

A fifth-generation Californian of Mexican and Native American (Chumasch) heritage, **Lorna Dee Cervantes** has been a pivotal figure in the Chicano literary movement since the mid-1970s, when she began publishing *Mango*, a literary journal, and founded the publishing company of the same name. Cervantes's own first book, *Emplumada* (University of Pittsburgh, 1981), was followed by *From the Cables of Genocide: Poems on Love and Hunger* (Arte Público, 1991), which was awarded the Patterson Poetry Prize and the poetry prize of the Institute of Latin American Writers. She holds an A.B.D. in the History of Consciousness. After completing a year-long Visiting Scholar Fellowship at the University of Houston, she has recently returned to the University of Colorado in Boulder, where she teaches creative writing. Cervantes is a founding co-editor of *Red Dirt,* a literary magazine, and has received two poetry fellowships from the National Endowment for the Arts.

Born in Las Cruces, New Mexico, **Denise Chávez**'s plays and stories focus on small-town life in the Chihuahuan desert. She is the author of a collection of short fiction, *The Last of the Menu Girls* (Arte Público Press, 1986), the title story of which was included in *The Norton Anthology of American Literature,* and her most recent work is the novel *Face of an Angel* (Farrar, Straus & Giroux, 1994). Chávez is the author of dozens of plays which have been produced throughout the United States and Europe, including productions at the Edinburgh Festival and the Festival Latino de Nueva York (through Joseph Papp).

Chávez holds a M.A. in creative writing from the University of New Mexico and a M.F.A. in drama from Trinity University. An accomplished actress, Chávez has toured her one-woman play, *Women in a State of Grace,* throughout the U.S. She has been a professor of drama at the University of Houston and has held various writer-in-residence positions. In 1989 she traveled across the Soviet Union as a delegate to the International Arts Commission sponsored by the Forum for U.S.–Soviet Dialogue. Currently, Chávez writes and teaches in her hometown of Las Cruces, New Mexico.

Sandra Cisneros is the leading Latina writer in the world in terms of sales, visibility, and critical reception. Born in Chicago, Cisneros received her M.F.A. from the University of Iowa Writers Workshop. She has lived off and on in San Antonio since 1984, when she became the director of the literature program for the Guadalupe Cultural Arts Center, and in 1985 she co-founded the Annual Texas Small Press Bookfair. Extremely popular as a lecturer and creative writing teacher, Cisneros has been writer-in-residence at universities all over the U.S.

The author of three collections of poetry and two of short fiction, Cisneros's books have been translated into ten languages. Her poetry is collected in *Bad Boys* (Mango Press, 1980), *My Wicked Wicked Ways* (Third Woman Press, 1987), and *Loose Woman* (Knopf, 1994). At the invitation of poet laureate Gwendolyn Brooks, Cisneros read her poetry at the Library of Congress in 1986; in 1995 she returned at the invitation of poet laureate Rita Dove. *The House on Mango Street* (1985) was long one of Arte Público's best-selling titles, and *Woman Hollering Creek* (Random House, 1991) was awarded the PEN Center West Award for fiction, the Quality Paperback Book Club New Voices Award, the Anisfield-Wolf Book Award, and the Lannan Foundation Literary Award. "The Eyes of Zapata" is from *Woman Hollering Creek.*

Cisneros was selected as a 1995 MacArthur Fellow, and is currently at work on her first novel entitled *Caramelo.*

Judith Ortiz was born in Hormigüeros, Puerto Rico, the daughter of a Navy man who moved his family back and forth between the island and Peterson, New Jersey. The family moved to Augusta, Georgia, in 1968. She earned her M.A. at Florida Atlantic University and did graduate work on scholarship at Oxford University.

Ortiz Cofer began writing poetry after college, and after four early chapbooks were published, her two collections *Reaching for the Mainland* (Bilingual Review Press, 1987) and *Terms of Survival* (Arte Público, 1987) came out in 1987. Her poems have been widely anthologized. *Silent Dancing: A Remembrance of a Puerto Rican Childhood* (Arte Público, 1990) received a PEN American/Albrand special citation and was named a "Best Book for the Teen Years" by the New York Public Library. The title essay was included in the *1991 Best American Essays* anthology, edited by Joyce Carol Oates. Another essay included in this collection, "More Room," was included in the *Pushcart Prize* anthology. Ortiz Cofer's autobiographical novel, *The Line of the Sun* (University of Georgia Press, 1990), earned her critical acclaim and *The Latin Deli: Prose and Poetry* (University of Georgia Press, 1993) received the Anisfield-Wolf Award. The story included here, "Nada," appeared in *The Latin Deli* and received an O. Henry Award in 1994. Cofer's latest work is *An Island Like You: Stories of the Barrio* (Orchard, 1995).

Currently, Ortiz Cofer is a professor of English and Creative Writing at the University of Georgia and an associate staff member of the Bread Loaf Writers Conference.

Lucha Corpi was born in Jáltipan, Veracruz, Mexico, spent her teens in San Luis Potosí, and immigrated to the United States with her husband at age nineteen. She became both vice-chair of the Chicano Studies Executive Committee and coordinator of the Chicano Studies Library in 1970 at the University of California at Berkeley, and was a founding member of Aztlán Cultural.

Corpi's poetry was first collected in 1976 in *Fireflight: Three Latin American Poets*. Corpi's translator for that book, Catherine Rodríguez-Nieto, has since worked with the poet to produce two more award-winning collections, *Palabras de Mediodía/Noon Words* (El Fuego de Azatlan Publications, 1980) and *Variaciones Sobre una Tempestad/Variations on a Storm* (Third Woman Press, 1990). While Corpi writes her poetry in Spanish, all of her fiction has been written in English. The novels *Delia's Song* (Arte Público Press, 1984) and *Eulogy for a Brown Angel* (Arte Público Press, 1992) are both set in the turbulent early days of the movimiento in California. *Eulogy* features one of Latina literature's only detectives, Gloria Damasco, who has reappeared in Corpi's latest novel, *Cactus Blood* (Arte Público Press, 1995). "Four, Free and Illegal" is part of an unpublished collection of essays entitled *The Orphan and the Bookburner.*

Angela de Hoyos was born in Coahuila, Mexico, and has lived most of her life in San Antonio, Texas. Deeply affected by the Chicano political movement—and especially the Texas farm workers' struggle—in the late 1960s and early 1970s, de Hoyos's work is often cited as among the first fruits of the Chicano literary movement. Her books include *Arise Chicano! and Other Poems* (Backstage Books, 1975), *Chicano Poems: For the Barrio* (Backstage Books, 1975), *Poems/Poemas* (Buenos Aires, 1975), *Selecciones* (Xalapa, 1976), *Selected Poems/Selecciones* (Dezkalzp Press, 1977), and *Woman, Woman* (Arte Público, 1985). De Hoyos's poems have appeared in hundreds of literary magazines and in dozens of anthologies, including the *Longman Anthology of World Literature by Women* (Longman, 1989). Her work has been translated into fifteen languages and has been honored with awards in Argentina, India, Italy, Germany, and the United States. In this country, two book-length studies of de Hoyos's writing have been published: *The Multi-Faceted Poetic World of Angela de Hoyos* (Relampago Press, 1985) by Marcella Aguilar-Henson and *Angela de Hoyos: A Critical Look* (Pajarito Publications, 1979) by Luis Arturo Ramos. In 1993, de Hoyos was recognized by the National Association of Chicano Studies for her contributions to Chicano letters. At the 1994 San Antonio Poetry Festival she received a Lifetime Achievement Award and recognition by the Texas Commission on the Arts executive director Jean Paul Baptiste for de Hoyos's "profound contributions to the arts." De Hoyos is the publisher and editor of M&A Editions and of *Huehuetitlan,* a journal of Chicano culture and poetry. She is also a painter and graphic artist.

Born and raised in Los Angeles, **Margarita Engle** is the daughter of a Cuban mother and an American father, a visual artist. She has published two novels, *Singing to Cuba* (Arte Público Press, 1993) and *Sky Writing: A Novel of Cuba* (Bantam, 1995). Engle maintains a dual career as a fiction writer and journalist. Her opinion columns have been syndicated on a regular basis since 1982 to over two hundred newspapers, and she has published short stories in several major journals and nonfiction articles in such national magazines as *Vista, Hispanic, South American Explorer,* and *Garden,* among others. Trained as an agronomist and botanist, Engle worked as an irrigation specialist in southern California until 1990, and now lives in California with her husband and children.

Rosario Ferré was born in Ponce, Puerto Rico. In 1970 she started the Puerto Rican literary magazine *Zona de Carga y Descarga,* and after publishing her first book of short stories, *Papeles de Pandora* (1976), Ferré became the literary critic for *El Mundo.* She obtained her Ph.D. in Latin American literature from the University of Maryland, and has held visiting professorships at the University of California at Berkeley, Johns Hopkins University, Rutgers University, and elsewhere. Several of Ferré's twenty-plus books have been published in Mexico, including *Sitio a Eros* (1982), a collection of feminist essays, *Fábulas de la Garza Desangrada* (1984), a collection of poetry, and *Maldito Amor* (1986), a novel which was published in the United States as *Sweet Diamond Dust* (Ballantine, 1989). "The Glass Box" is from Ferré's short story collection *The Youngest Doll* (University of Nebraska, 1991). A new novel, *The House on the Lagoon,* is due out in 1995, and another, *Eccentric Neighborhoods,* will be, published in 1996; both are from Farrar, Straus & Giroux.

San Antonio poet and short story writer **Sheila Sánchez Hatch** has published her work in several literary magazines and in two anthologies, *Linking Roots* (M&A Editions, 1993) and *Mujeres Grandes I* (M&A Editions, 1993), and has edited a collection of work by North Texas Latinos, *Tierra Norte* (M&A Editions, 1994). She holds a M.F.A. from Vermont College and currently teaches English for the Alamo Community College District in San Antonio.

María Hinojosa is an award-winning journalist and news correspondent for National Public Radio and host of "Latino USA," a radio journal of news and culture, and "Visiones" on WNBC-TV. She is the author of *Crews: New York Gang Members Talk with María Hinojosa* (Harcourt Brace, 1995), based on a prize-winning news story. She is a recipient of the Robert F. Kennedy Award in Journalism, and lives in New York with her husband, photographer German Perez.

Maya Islas was born in Cabaiguán, Las Villas, Cuba, and came to the United States in 1965. In 1972 she received her B.A. in Psychology from Fairleigh Dickinson University and, in 1978, her M.A. in General Psychology from Montclair State College. In 1980, after serving as a bilingual teacher in New York City's public schools, Islas started working as a counselor for the Higher Education Opportunity Program at Elizabeth Seton College in New York, and co-founded, along with José Corrales and Mireya Robles, the literary magazine *Palabras y Papel* in 1981. She was writer-in-residence in 1989 at the School of Design, Altos de

Chavón, Dominican Republic, where she taught psychology with a visual arts focus.

Islas has published several books of poetry, including *Without a Name* (1974), *Sombras Papel/Shadows-Paper* (1978), *Hubo la Viola* (1979), *Altazora Accompanying Vincent* (1989), *Merla* (1991), and *Blackbird* (1993). She received the Silver Caravelle Award in Poetry from Barcelona in 1978 for the poem "Words of the Dove," the 1986 Gold Letters Award from the University of Miami for *Altazora Accompanying Vincent,* and the 1993 Latino Literature Prize in Poetry for *Blackbird.*

Inés Martínez is a native of New Mexico and a professor of English literature at Kingsborough Community College in Brooklyn, New York, where she has lived for over twenty years. In 1993, Martínez established Sandia Press and published her first novel, *To Know the Moon* (Sandia Press), a psychological exploration of the relationship between an ill mother and her lesbian daughter. "The Singing Antelope," included in this anthology, won the 1987 New York Foundation for the Arts Fellowship for Fiction.

A critic and reviewer, **Bryce Milligan** is the author of five historical novels and short-story collections for young adults, including the award-winning *With the Wind, Kevin Dolan* (Corona Publishing, 1987). He has also written three collections of poetry—*Daysleepers & Other Poems* (Corona, 1984), *Litany Sung at Hell's Gate* (M&A Editions, 1991), and *Working the Stone* (Wings Press, 1994)—five plays, and numerous articles on Latino/Latina literature. Milligan is the founding editor of *Pax: A Journal for Peace Through Culture* and *Vortex: A Critical Review.* He is the cofounder, with Sandra Cisneros, of the San Antonio Inter-American Bookfair. Currently, Milligan is the director of the literature program at the Guadalupe Cultural Arts Center in San Antonio, where his recently directed the first annual *"Hijas del Quito Sol*: Studies in Latina Identity" conference. Milligan and Mary Guerrero Milligan, his wife of twenty years, live in San Antonio with their two children, two cats, and fifteen thousand books.

A native of San Antonio, **Mary Guerrero Milligan** studied history and journalism and took her M.L.S. from the University of North Texas, where she was the recipient of several student writing awards. She has served as librarian for St. Luke's Episcopal School for ten years, where she has hosted many notable writers, and she regularly presents programs and workshops on multicultural children's literature at conferences around the country and for regional librarians and teachers. She has long served as the manuscript reader and editor for Corona Publishing Company of San Antonio, and has written reviews for the *Albuquerque Journal, the San Antonio Express News,* and for various literary magazines and journals. She was a regular essayist, story translator, and interviewer for the journal *Pax.*

Guerrero's most recent publications include short stories in *Blue Mesa's Review* and *Huehuetitlan,* an annotated bibliography of Latino children's literature in *Texas Journal,* and a one-act play published in the anthology *Mujeres Grandes I.*

Pat Mora was born and raised in El Paso, where she lived, taught, and served in various top administrative capacities at the University of Texas at El Paso until moving to Cincinnati, Ohio in 1989. A Kellogg National Fellowship in 1986 allowed her to study national and international cultural conservation issues. Called "the most widely anthologized Latina poet in this country," Mora and her work have received numerous awards and honors, including two Southwest Book Awards and a National Endowment for the Arts poetry fellowship. Mora's poetry collections include *Chants, Borders,* and *Communion* (Arte Público, 1984, 1986, and 1991, respectively) and *Agua Santa/Holy Water* (Beacon, 1995). She is also the author of a collection of personal essays, *Nepantla: Essays from the Land in the Middle* (University of New Mexico Press, 1993). The mother of three children, Mora is the author of such works of children's literature as *A Birthday Basket for Tía* (Macmillan, 1992), *Listen to the Desert/Oye al Deserto* (Clarion, 1994), *Pablo's Tree* (Macmillan, 1994), *The Desert is My Mother* (Piñata Books/Arte Público, 1994), *A Gift of Poinsettias* (Piñata Books/Arte Público, 1995), and *The Race of Toad and Deer* (Orchard, 1995).

A native of Los Angeles, Latina activist **Cherríe Moraga** is a poet, playwright, editor, and essayist. A founding editor of Kitchen Table: Women of Color Press, Moraga is the co-editor (with Gloria Anzaldúa) of *This Bridge Called My Back: Writings by Radical Women of Color* (Persephone Press, 1981), as well as *Cuentos: Stories by Latinas* (Kitchen Table: Women of Color Press, 1983), *Giving Up the Ghost: Teatro in Two Acts* (West End Press, 1986), and *The Last Generation* (South End Press, 1993). Moraga has been the recipient of fellowships from the National Endowment for the

Arts and the Fund for New American Plays. She has taught at the University of California at Berkeley for several years.

Deborah Paredez, a native of San Antonio, has been publishing poems since the age of fifteen. As a young writer, she was included several times in *Young Pegasus* anthologies, the oldest student poetry publication in the U.S. She attended Trinity University, where she served as the editor of the university's literary magazine. Paredez is currently working on her Ph.D. in Latino theater at Northwestern University.

Born in Belo Horizonte, Brazil, **Teresinka Pereira** has lived in the United States since 1960. In 1985, she was the recipient of the Noble Title of Dame of Magistral Grace from Dom Waldemar Baroni Santos, Prince of Brazil, for her literary merits. In 1972, she was awarded the National Prize for Theater in Brazil. Pereira has been a member of the Academia Norteamericana de la Lengua Española, and a correspondent of the Royal Spanish Academy since 1989. She is a member of the Governing Board of the World Congress of Poets and the Research Board of Advisors of the American Biographical Institute. Pereira is President of the International Writers & Artists Association, which she founded in the 1970s. Her poetry and essays have been translated into more than twenty languages. She is a professor of Spanish and Hispanic American Literature at Bluffton College, Ohio.

Before she began her career as a novelist, **Cecile Pineda** was the founder and director of the experimental theater company Theater of Man in San Francisco. She is the author of *Face* (Viking, 1984), which won the Sue Kaufman Prize for First Fiction from the American Academy and Institute of Arts and Letters and a gold medal from the Commonwealth Club of California, and was nominated for a National Book Award. Pineda is also the author of the novels *Frieze* (Viking, 1985) and *The Love Queen of the Amazon* (Little, Brown, 1993). Born and raised in New York City, Pineda is currently Visiting Writer at San Diego State University.

Born in San Antonio, of Mexican and German descent, **Nicole Pollentier** is the youngest contributor to *Daughters of the Fifth Sun*. She is currently an undergraduate at Brown University. She has been included in several issues of the *Young Pegasus* anthology, in three issues of *Hanging*

Loose, in several San Antonio literary magazines, and has received prizes from Palo Alto College, San Antonio, and from the C. W. Miller Poetry Contest, Trinity University.

Born in Artemisa, Cuba, **Eliana Suárez Rivero** has lived in the United States since 1967. She obtained her Ph.D. at the University of Miami, Florida. She is a noted scholar of contemporary Hispanic American poetry, particularly the work of Pablo Neruda. Currently she is a professor of Spanish literature at the University of Arizona in Tucson. Her book *El Gran Amor de Pablo Neruda: Estudio Crítico de su Poesía* (1975) was published in Spain. Her poetry has been included in numerous anthologies and magazines and in her own collections, *Cuerpos Breves/Brief Bodies* (Arizona, 1976) and *De cal y arena* (1975). She co-edited *Siete Poetas/Seven Poets* (with Margarita Cota-Cárdena, Scorpion Books, 1978) and *Infinite Divisions: An Anthology of Chicana Literature* (with Tey Diana Rebolledo, University of Arizona Press, 1994). Suárez Rivero is currently working on a study of U.S. Latino literature and a collection of autobiographical essays.

Born in Guantánamo, Cuba, **Mireya Robles** came to the United States in 1957. She received a B.A. in English at Russell Sage College (1966), a M.A. at the State University of New York, Albany (1968), and her Ph.D. at the State University of New York, Stony Brook (1975).

Robles's first novel, *Hagiografía de Narcisa la Bella,* was published by Ediciones del Norte in 1985. Her award-winning anthology, *Tiempo Artesano/Time the Artisan* (translated by Angela de Hoyos), was published by M&A Editions in 1977. Robles currently teaches Spanish and literature at the University of Natal, South Africa, where she is Senior Lecturer in the Spanish Department.

Carmen Tafolla's latest book, *Sonnets to Human Beings* (Lalo Press, 1995), won the University of California at Irvine's 1989 National Chicano Literature Contest. She is also the author of *To Split a Human: Mitos, Machos y la Mujer Chicana* (Mexican-American Cultural Center, 1985) and the poetry collection *Curandera* (M&A Editions, 1983). Born in San Antonio, Tafolla has been a professor of women's studies at the University of California at Fresno, and special assistant to the president of Northern Arizona University. She currently lives in McAllen, Texas, where she is at work on a novel.

Gloria Vando's first collection of poetry, *Promesas: Geography of the Impossible* (Arte Público, 1993) was preceded by numerous appearances in some of the top U.S. literary magazines. *Promesas* won the 1994 Thorp Menn Award for Poetry. Vando earned her B.A. at Texas A&I, Corpus Christi, and attended New York University, the University of Amsterdam, and the Academie Julian in Paris. In 1991 Vando won the Billee Murray Denny Poetry Prize; other awards include the Kansas Fellowship in Poetry (the first granted by the state), a CCLM Editors Grant, and the Barbara Deming Memorial Award.

Vando is founder and editor of *The Helicon Nine Reader,* an anthology featuring the best of *Helicon Nine,* which won the 1991 Governor's Arts Award (Kansas). She is also co-founder of The Writers Place, a literary resource center for writers and readers. She presently lives in Kansas City, where she publishes Helicon Nine Editions.

Enedina Cásarez Vásquez, an artist, poet, playwright, and short story writer, is the author of the collection *Recuerdos de una Niña* (Centro de Comunicación Misioneros Oblatos de María, 1980) and such plays as *Te Traigo estas Flores y Marshmallow Peeps, The Visit,* and *La Virgen de San Juan de los Lagos.* She is a founding member of the performance/writing group Mujeres Grandes and a noted folk artist, whose iconographic *nichos* are included in the permanent collections of several major museums, including the Smithsonian Institution. Vásquez has been awarded the Hidalgo Award and the Empressario Award de San Antonio, and is a member of the San Antonio Women's Hall of Fame. A former poet-in-residence of the Texas Commission on the Arts, she now teaches creative writing in San Antonio.

Shortly after she won the Coordinating Council of Literary Magazines' national poetry contest in 1976 for her feminist poem, "Ay qué ritmo," **Evangelina Vigil-Piñon**'s first collection of poems, *Thirty an' Seen a Lot* (Arte Público Press, 1982), was published and received an American Book Award from the Before Columbus Foundation. She has also been the recipient of a poetry fellowship from the National Endowment for the Arts and has been recognized by the national Association of Chicano Studies for her work. Vigil-Piñon is the author of the poetry collection *The Computer is Down* (Arte Público, 1987), the editor of a pioneering anthology of Latina writing, *Woman of Her Word* (Arte Público Press, 1983) and the translator of Tomás Rivera's classic novel . . . *And the Earth Did Not Devour Him* (Arte Público, 1992).

Born and raised in the San Francisco Mission District, **Alma Luz Villanueva** is of Yaqui, Spanish, and German ancestry. Her first book of poetry, *Bloodroot* (Place of Herons Press) was published in 1977, the same year her manuscript "Poems" won the Chicano Literary Prize at the University of California at Irvine. Villanueva's first novel, *The Ultraviolet Sky* (Bilingual Review Press, 1988), was the recipient of the American Book Award of the Before Columbus Foundation and has recently been re-issued by Anchor Doubleday. Her second novel, *Naked Ladies,* was published by Bilingual Review Press in 1994. Other poetry collections include *Mother, May I?* (Motheroot Publications, 1978), *Life Span* (Place of Herons Press, 1984), *La Chingada* (Bilingual Review Press, 1985), and *Planet* (Bilingual Review Press, 1993), which won the Latin American Writers Institute Award in poetry. Her most recent book is *Weeping Woman: La Llorona and Other Stories* (Bilingual Review Press, 1995).

Villanueva, who holds a M.F.A. in Writing from Vermont College at Norwich University, teaches creative writing at the University of California, Santa Cruz.

Restless Serpents (Diseños Literarios, 1976), **Bernice Zamora**'s first book of poetry, is a collaborative collection of poems written with José Antonio Burciaga. *Releasing Serpents,* her second collection, was published by Bilingual Review Press in 1994. Zamora received her Ph.D. in English and American Studies from Stanford University in 1986. She teaches literature and writing at Santa Clara University.